The Mental Side of Golf

Charles M. Bonasera

TRIAD
Publishing Group

Sarasota, Florida

TRIAD
Publishing Group

For information regarding permissions, write to
The TRIAD Publishing Group: Publisher, 3233 Ramblewood Dr N, Sarasota, FL 34237.

ISBN 13: 978-0-9801373-7-8
ISBN 10: 0-9801373-7-3
Printed in the U.S.A.
Printed December, 2007

Table of Contents

Dedication

The person to whom I want to dedicate this work never played golf; she had never even swung a club in her lifetime. In fact, she never played a sport in her life but thoroughly enjoyed watching others play. She had a very sharp mind and an outstanding imagination. She also had a remarkable ability to break down a person's movements, while they were doing something, into small pieces, which would help others become more aware of their steps and how to improve their whole performance. This ability was the result of the painful process she underwent in the course of doing the simplest of tasks. She communicated easily with everyone and although she had a bit of a temper, I preferred to call that facet her spirit.

When she was young, she wore braces on both her legs. When older, she accomplished all of her tasks from a wheelchair. She was stricken with polio at the tender age of eight and remained affected throughout her whole body until her death. The infection returned, which ultimately rendered her totally helpless, except for her mind. Her mind, even despite mini-strokes that she suffered as well as a number of other maladies, remained strong and functional until her death.

Despite all of these problems and handicaps, she remained positive and purposeful throughout her life and became a role model for the many people with whom she came into contact. For me, she was more than just a role model. She was my mentor. I could argue points with her without feeling rejected as a child and although I became her helper; her presence in my life became my guiding principle upon which I depend to this day. She was my best friend growing up and even now, despite not being with us anymore, I can still feel her presence, influence, love and support.

Her most famous saying in response to the physical pain that she experienced throughout her lifetime was, "And this too shall pass." She taught me about pain and endurance. She taught me about living life to the fullest. She taught me to believe in myself and what I do. She taught me never to give up no matter what the odds. Rather than depend on others, she would perform tasks that seemed to take an inordinate amount of time but were really a testimonial to her sense of independence and stamina.

I am talking about my sister, Jo. I miss her. I miss her terribly but she will never leave my mind. This book epitomizes many of the techniques and qualities that she possessed without any formal training. She learned how to relax her muscles, which were stricken with that horrible disease so that she could painfully perform simple tasks. She used imagery and visualization to entertain herself in her mind, despite her body's inability to perform those feats. She had an enjoyable sense of humor and a beautiful and infectious laugh.

My professional mentor was Dr. Milton Erickson, who was a famous hypnotherapist, psychiatrist and psychotherapist. He too was stricken with polio at a very young age and literally taught himself to walk out of pure self-determination. He would say that if you are handicapped, you must adopt the obsessive attitude of "I'm going to do this or die." He worked with many athletes, many of whom were of Olympic caliber, who came to him for help in their performance despite his handicap. Of him it was said that out of a wheelchair he won Olympic championships all the time. My sister was of similar mind and if you met either of these people you would be inspired beyond your imagination to succeed and do the right thing for yourself. It is all about how we use our mind.

I want those who read this book to capture the same inspiration and motivation that my sister and Dr. Erickson epitomized. Above all, they both taught me to enjoy life and enjoy it thoroughly. I am grateful to them and now that I have introduced them to you. As you read on, you will be trained to relax your mind in order to begin using ingenuity, visualization and imagery. You will be helped to gain a sense of confidence in order to combat fears and believe in yourself so that you can take the risks that result in growth. You will be helped to develop an effective use of your mind and to have the determination and imagination to create new ways around obstacles that occur both on the golf course and in your life as well.

I trust that you will enjoy this book as much as they enjoyed living their lives and I enjoyed writing it.

Forward

I was very pleased when my long time friend, Charlie Bonasera, asked me to write the forward to his latest book, The Mental Side of Golf. I thought about the time in 1966 when we participated in a monthly discussion club among diverse professionals. Charlie and I were of like mind and we enjoyed playing some fun mind games with the group. I wondered whether Charlie was going to play similar mind games with his readers.

Then I read the draft manuscript. Clearly, he is not playing mind games with his readers. Instead, he is teaching his readers how to create their own mind games as an important part of their enjoyment of the game of golf. Early on in his book, Charlie says that

"Once a golfer:

1. Gains a basic understanding of the fundamentals of golf,
2. Learns to train and control his/her mind and body to execute various shots,
3. Maintains a solid working practice routine, and
4. Finally develops a feel for his/her performance while playing, he/she will then be able to form good golfing habits and shoot well."

His four points are an excellent description of how to succeed in any endeavor, whether in golf or in life. Then

I thought about the last time that we played golf together to see whether he really practices what he preaches. The course we played in Florida is best described as 18 water holes that are linked together to form a cruel maze. Every hole has at least one shot across water with alligators and most holes have two and even three such shots. It was very early morning and the sun was barely visible because of a dense fog that covered the whole area.

The first tee looks out over the water. We both envisioned high drives that carried 165 yards, which put us in the middle of the fairway with only a wedge shot remaining to the green. We both hit wonderful drives and I was away, which meant that I would be first to be on the green in regulation.

I envisioned a soft high pitch to the green, which would land below the flag and roll to within ten feet of the cup for my first birdie attempt of the day. After a short practice swing, I took my stance and promptly shanked the ball into the lake. As Charlie laughed, I shrugged my shoulders and tried removing that experience from my mind. Then Charlie hit his ball into one of the sand traps and our round began. We both scored a double bogey on the first hole.

We laughed together as we rode our cart to the second tee. The second tee looked out between stands of pine trees on either side of the fairway. There was a pond on the left side of the fairway just after the narrow passage through the trees. There was an eight foot alligator sunning itself on the bank of the pond. We both said that we didn't have to worry about it because we would probably slice the ball off the tee. It was Charlie's honor but he had to go back to the previous hole to find a club that he thought he left behind. Actually, he mistakenly put his club in my bag.

We both laughed again when he returned to the tee. I had already hit my drive and was in the center of the fairway. Charlie addressed his ball. He played for a gentle fade but instead hit a streaming line drive straight at the alligator. We watched his ball hit the alligator's head causing the alligator to run into the lake. His ball caromed off the alligator and landed in the fairway about five yards ahead of my drive. We gave each other high fives and laughed as we drove to our balls for the next shot. We both scored our first and last par on the second hole.

The remaining sixteen holes were similar to the first two. We both broke 100. We lost some balls but found others to replace them. As we drove home to meet our wives we talked about the experience that we just enjoyed. I am reminded of the advice that my mother-in-law gave me years ago. She said, "Since you can be happy or you can be sad, you might as well be happy."

We were happy. When we came home, our wives asked us about our golfing experience and our response was, "We did great! We came away with a net gain of three balls and Charlie hit an alligator." I wonder if our recent golf experience is one of the reasons that he decided to write a book about the mental side of golf. Read his book and see what you think.

William Roy Kesting
President and Founder
Kesting Ventures® Corp

Preface

Apart from my professional credentials in presenting this material, the rest are simple. My father, who played semi-professional baseball and was an avid fan of the game, greatly influenced my interest in sports. I played baseball and basketball, pond and organized hockey as well as sandlot football. I coached, refereed, umpired and managed basketball, hockey and baseball teams. I began playing golf at the age of twenty-eight and still play this wonderful game.

When I consult with people to help them resolve their personal issues, I focus on how their thoughts and feelings are affecting their lives as well as the patterns they use to deal with life. Then, we determine which patterns are effective and those that are not and work toward changing those that aren't. I use the same techniques for the mental side of sports. Apart from the technical aspects of sports, I became aware that the manner in which athletes use their minds actually affects their performance. That is why I gradually devoted a part of my practice to working with professional and amateur athletes and coaches in a number of different sports.

I worked with figure skaters, tennis players, gymnasts, Olympic skiers, equestrians, swimmers, divers, track and field athletes, golfers, amateur and professional hockey players and coaches. One of the groups I worked with was the Buffalo Sabres, NHL Professional Hockey Team, just prior to the playoffs portion of their season. I helped them reduce stress and improve the mental side of their sport as well as their performance through the use of imagery and visualization.

There are many people, who I want to thank for their help and encouragement in scripting this presentation. First of all, my devoted wife, Barbara, whose patience with my frequent absences in our relationship allowed me the time to prepare this work. Roy Kesting's suggestions, recommendations and editing were invaluable and provided a much needed change in perspective. My newfound friend, Jack O'Malley and my beloved daughter, Christina, were extremely helpful in editing the material as well. They afforded me a second and third look at both the content and the manner in which it is presented. Paula Shingfield's keen eye for sentence meaning was also very helpful to the process.

I also want to thank my sons, Joe and Chuck, to whom I gave their first lesson in golf at the ages of eleven and nine. I showed them how to hold a club and address the ball and then I said, "Hit it." Without any effort, they did and they have been hitting it well ever since without ever taking another lesson to my knowledge. They are both excellent golfers.

What comes naturally to the young is what adults need to work at regaining.

I note here that my references to comments made by professional golfers in this presentation were taken from television interviews they conducted during and after play and/or T.V. specials during the 2006 golf season. I took notes of their comments to support the points I have made.

Attempts were made to inform everyone mentioned in this book of the usage of their names and comments as well as the T.V. networks (ABC, NBC, and CBS) that carried tournament play. Also, references to different athletic endeavors are cited in order to help golfers determine how those lessons can be applied to their golfing performance.

There is a mental side to every sport and athletic endeavor and that everyone's mental side is different.

Also, it is very important to note here that there are many suggestions that I will make over the course of this book. Please do not try practicing all of them at once. Otherwise, you will become overwhelmed and the value of whatever it is you want to achieve will be lost. Instead, practice one suggestion at a time, until you are satisfied that you have accomplished whatever the goal is that you wish to achieve, before going onto the next suggestion. Take your time and be patient with yourself and your progress will ultimately pay off one-hundred-fold.

I will be repeating some concepts and suggestions in different sections of the book because of their significance and importance. These repetitions will take place in different contexts to solidify your understanding and practice of whatever those points might be. There are some things in life that deserve repetition.

"No one taught me how to play this game.
No one taught me how to hold a club.
No one taught me how to sink a thirteen foot putt
to win the President's Cup
No one had to."

TV commercial excerpt featuring Chris DeMarco

 # Introduction:
How I Got Started.

The issues and suggestions made in this book with respect to the game of golf were designed to also serve readers and listeners as a guide to the process of life management. Although spending over forty years as a psychotherapist, I have always enjoyed sports of all kinds. I began working with athletes in many different sports in the mid-80's as a result of my daughter's figure skating coach asking me to work with a group of her students.

Her concerns were many and varied. Most of the students came into skating at a very young age because of the glamour associated with the sport. For many, skating was a social environment in which lasting friends and enemies could be made. The sport is based in some very intense competitive moves that each skater must perform in a program, which are then evaluated by a panel of serious and judgmental adults. Each skater is then given a place in their group's order based on the scores they received with the top three in each group receiving honors. Oftentimes, the competition resulted in skaters turning on one another to interrupt their mental focus, instead of remaining focused on their own performance.

In effect, they didn't really realize what competition is intended to achieve. They took everything personally, as children have a tendency to do, and the stress and pressure on them was devastating at times. It not only affected the skaters in their skating programs but their personal lives as well. In some instances, there were some pretty serious problems that came about in their family relationships.

There is a great deal of pressure and stress associated with skating competition and the students were very fearful of the whole process.

I formed one group and started working with them and then that evolved into working with different age and skill groups, which were referred to me by various other coaches. My role was to help them deal with the mental side of their sport and their emotions and perception of themselves while they were performing their sport. A great deal of emphasis was also placed on teaching them how to rebound after making mistakes in their program. I have devoted a part of this book to that same concept and the tools that will allow golfers to come back after they hit a bad shot.

My work caught on and referrals of many athletes of different age groups and sports resulted. My work with them consisted of helping them understand how their mind worked and how the use of their minds would determine how well or poorly they would perform. I correlated how the manner in which they used their mind affected their thinking, emotions and their psyche as well. I also helped them understand that how they conducted their personal lives could carry over into their sport.

The major points that I stress during my work with athletes and discuss in this book deal with:

- maintaining focus,
- personal endurance,
- positive thinking,
- dealing with making mistakes and being able to

rebound from them,
- building confidence,
- personal slumps,
- personal fears,
- the carryover effect,
- the nature of competition,
- personal expectations as well as the expectations of others, and finally,
- effectively dealing with success and failure.

I place the greatest emphasis on helping athletes recognize and deal with their thoughts and feelings, especially those that interfere with their performance.

I have used the reference of figure skating realizing that this sport is far different from the game/sport of golf. However, the elements noted above apply to all sports regardless of differences in their nature. Although the manner in which athletes compete in different sports may not be the same, competition is still competition. The mental side of all sports concerns the manner in which all athletes use their minds to compete successfully. Golfers should learn to adapt these principles to their sense of being in competition, whether with opponents or themselves.

One of the main methods that I use to help athletes attain a working sense of their performance is to train them in deep relaxation, imagery and visualization to teach them how to use their entire brain for their sports activities. This helps transfer what they envision their performance to be into an actual experience in the course of performing their sport. I will be training you in a similar method later on in this book.

People learn in different ways, in their own style and at their own pace.

Before ending with this section of the book, I want to briefly say something about the process of learning. The problem that educators and parents experience is that they frequently believe that learning must take place in a structured manner. They assume that whatever is being taught is able to be understood and used similarly by all students. This is the one size fits all approach to education. Nothing could be further from the truth.

When someone explains something to you, you should translate the lesson into your own language. The instructor's words and concepts are just that, the instructor's words and concepts. Memorization alone does not guarantee that you actually understand or have learned how to use the lesson.

Learning may result from reading and exposure to new concepts and methods but knowledge can only come from experiencing them.

Then, in order to absorb the knowledge you need to solve this problem in the future, you must first understand the steps you need to go through to find the solutions for yourself. Therefore, don't take my words as gospel. Rather, have your own words become your gospel.

The Opening Scene

Imagine the following scenario: It's a beautiful day. The sun is shining brightly and you have finally taken some time off to play golf with some of your friends who have been after you for some time to play a round of golf. Consider that you are a perfectionist and a competitor and although you believe in the saying that a bad day on the links is better than a good day in the office, it doesn't always work out that way. You are a little rusty so you decide to see a golf instructor to refresh your swing fundamentals and overall game. You even purchase some new clubs, which you feel will improve your game. You go to the driving range and practice for a couple of hours. You are all set or so you think.

You have tried to commit everything the pro taught you to memory. Your swing, stance and everything else should result in being able to hit that little white ball a country mile. You are the last to tee off and you are nervous but butterflies are a good sign, or so you think. You remember to use correct tempo during your practice swing. Your stance and grip are just right. It is time for your round to begin. You address your ball, concentrate and take your first swing. As you are walking to retrieve your ball you talk to yourself saying: *"Darn it! You raised your head. Why can't I control my head? you ask yourself. Your ball ends up in the heavy rough bordering the woods but that's ok you say to yourself because at least the ball didn't go into* the woods. I need to be philosophical about this. It's only a game. Don't take it so seriously. Don't sweat the next shot. Those guys are probably watching me. I should be able to beat Jim. I always have in the past but he hit a perfect shot. Just relax! Come on, Relax! RELAX!"

You continue to talk to yourself.

"The grass is much longer than it looked like back there. What club should I use? Should I hit the ball with an open or closed face? Should I play for distance or play it safe? That branch could get in the way of my swing. My hands are sweating and I'm feeling really up tight, a lot more than nervous. Oh, what the heck, JUST DO IT!

SWISH, the ball only traveled about 15 feet into even heavier rough. My wrists hurt from swinging through that high grass. Boy am I out of shape! Sure enough, I hit the branch. I used the wrong club angle. That darned pro doesn't know what he's talking about! Maybe the next shot will be better. Maybe I should have put off this golf date until I had a little more practice. I certainly am not having any fun today and that's what playing with my friends is supposed to be all about. God, I hope that my bad luck won't continue. Maybe on the next hole my luck will change. But then again, maybe it won't. WHAT THEN?

I've got to get over that last hole but I can't shake what's just happened and this is just the first hole. Are they laughing at me? Why is my breathing so hard? Now I'm getting really angry. Somebody said it. I don't know who. It's only a game. It's only a game, and so on, and so on, and so on."

This scene sets the tone for the real purpose of this scenario. Many of us have been there at one time or another and some of us would rather not admit it. You have had the right instruction, the right clubs, and learned the right way of playing the game. Everything is there that should be there, but what about your mind? What about the mental side of golf? How important is that aspect? As you read this book, try to answer that question for yourself.

The book presumes that you have experienced and practiced some basic instruction in the fundamentals of the game of golf. I will not be instructing you on a technical basis and will only allude to technical aspects to give examples pertaining to the main theme; namely the mental side of golf. The secondary theme is to show how elements of golf play and the mental side of the game can also be applied to life management issues in our daily routines. I have found the connection to be fascinating. I hope that you will as well.

What Constitutes the Mental Side of Golf?

The word mental seems to have taken on a negative or threatening meaning in our society but I will be using this term to indicate the rational and creative thinking within your mind.

I will be emphasizing that your mind is the most important part of your physical being. You can learn to train your mind to control and minimize interfering thoughts, feelings and wasted activity. Thoughts that lead to troublesome feelings and performances that interfere with your golf game can be modified to benefit you

Later in this book, I'll teach you methods of picturing yourself swinging a club through the process of imagery and visualization. This training will include performing in slow motion as well. Your mind has a remarkable ability to incorporate new learning and can teach your body to do what it needs to do to play and enjoy the game of golf.

An interesting way to watch sports is to focus on what the athletes might be thinking and feeling while performing and how they deal with making mistakes. When possible, watch their eyes to gain a sense of their attitude, feelings and thoughts and how these affect their performance. Become preoccupied with the mental side of sports and then begin to take notice of the mental side of your golf game as well as how to use your mind to help you manage your life.

The "MENTAL SIDE" is characterized by:

1) Skill acquired by athletes in their play that has been gained from instruction, training and practice,

2) Emotional elements, which tend to facilitate or diminish performance,

3) An athlete's ability to maintain focus while playing his/her sport,

4) An athlete's ability to rebound after making a mistake instead of forming a negative attitude,

5) An athlete's ability to develop a working understanding of competition as it applies to his/her sport, and

6) An athlete's ability to develop a realistic emotional and behavioral sense of winning and losing.

Although there may be specific differences between individual and team sports, the mental principles apply to all competitive sports.

Left Brain... Right Brain

Now, I want to briefly familiarize you with the functions of the left and right sides of the brain. The left side's functions concern logic, sequencing, rational thought, analysis, objectivity and the ability to look at various parts of a task. The right side's functions concern random thought, intuition, bringing parts of a whole together, subjectivity and being able to perceive entire concepts. Try picturing thoughts going back and forth between the two sides of your brain while being influenced by each of these functions. Most people have a distinct preference for one of these styles of thinking. However, only a small number of people are adept at both modes of thought. Educational institutions tend to favor left-brain modes of thinking while downplaying the right-brain modes. Students are trained to focus on logical thinking, analysis, and accuracy. Right-brained subjects, on the other hand, focus on aesthetics, feeling, and creativity.

When we reflect on our experiences, we can construct our personal understanding and interpretation of what we have learned. The more personal understanding we have for what we have learned, the more knowledge we acquire. So, when a pro teaches us a new grip or a different swing, our ability to use that technique is dependent on our perception and not merely the pro's instructions. As individuals decipher their own meaning of what is being taught, learning and the acquisition of knowledge takes place, which we can then put to use. In other words, the pro's words must become your words. Practicing is necessary because it puts new learning into your personal experience. This is how your knowledge is formed.

This concept is vital to mastering the game of golf. Golfers are always competing with themselves to progress their skill in the sport.

The pressure of competition might produce many thoughts and feelings that interfere with your performance. The more aware of your thoughts, emotions and your mood you can be, the more capable you will be able to achieve your desired goal in a confident manner. Some of you may take notes while you're playing the game. Constant reminders can help improve performance and provide consistency to your efforts. The range of your preparation can go from a relatively relaxed attitude to a much more intense one depending on what works best for you.

Something should be said about beating the game to death. Sometimes people have a tendency to overthink what they are about to do to the point that their thoughts interferes with their performance. An example is the approach that a small child takes to learn a new task. A child does not focus and concentrate on thinking through the steps that are required to accomplish a task. Instead, the child jumps in and just does it. Granted, they may not be initially successful but their enthusiasm and sense of purpose tend to take over with their eye on accomplishing the task. For those who have natural abilities, their experience may be a successful one. For those who may not possess natural abilities, they might need more instruction, time and practice.

What is interesting to me is that despite the fact that

children may not be immediately successful and despite a child's tendency to experience immediate gratification, when children are really intent on accomplishing a goal, they will pursue it persistently until the goal is achieved.

I have witnessed this process in both young and older children. This is why I urge adults to think and act more like children when they are in an overthinking mode. In other words, I ask them to lighten up to help them understand that their thinking is inhibiting their success. I also recommend that they strive to have fun while they are doing something.

By the same token, there are some adults who need to go through their ritual of thinking to accomplish their goal. I find that their efforts are more intense and less enjoyable during their learning process. They get so serious that their incentive to continue tends to diminish because they feel that either the task is just too hard or their success is coming too slowly. In those cases, I work with the individual to teach him/her how to relax and enjoy what they are learning.

Usually the benefits of doing so become an incentive for them to give up their overthinking in favor of their enjoyment and progress. The more that you can focus on how you use your mind instead of just the technical aspects of golf, the greater your success rate will become at mastering a given technique.

Improving the mental approach to sports can be accomplished by everyone. There is no magic to it. It just requires a change of focus and outlook to use your mind to help you accomplish and enjoy almost any task.

This point is illustrated quite nicely by a human interest story that recently appeared on a morning news program. The story was about a youngster who plays golf. He is about four or five years old and in remission from cancer. While he was being treated for his illness he became interested in watching golf tournaments on TV. He spent all of his time watching The Golf Channel along with tournaments. He would also look at The Golf Magazine.

Neither of his parents plays golf but they encouraged their child to follow his interest because it calmed him while he was being treated. When he was well enough, his father took him to a golf course so that he could actually play golf. Surprisingly, the child was immediately able to hit the ball with a wonderfully executed golf swing. The TV report showed the boy playing golf and his golf swing was very impressive for someone that young who had never had any formal instruction. He was already scoring 36 for 9 holes.

The reporter went on to say that the child had lost one of his eyes because of the nature and severity of his illness. The reporter asked the child's father whether he played with his son and his father replied that he just caddied for the boy because he didn't know how to play golf. He also knew that his son wanted to play by himself so that he could play faster. The reporter asked the boy whether he thought that he would ever be able to beat Tiger Woods. The boy responded that he didn't see why he couldn't beat Tiger in the future because his ability was up to him.

You are able to do great things with your mind.

What About Golf?

I am frequently asked by both professional and amateur golfers to help them improve the mental aspects of their game. Recent studies performed with Olympic athletes indicate that mind training is both vital and necessary to their overall training. Playing golf well is much more than the implementation of technical training, possessing proper equipment or receiving instruction from a professional. Rather, it is the feel that we develop from our technical training in the use of the equipment. A feel for the game is our ability to play without having to go through a series of conscious steps to play well.

Initially, when learning something new, it is necessary to think about what you are doing and become aware of how you feel as you perform. However, as you continue to do so, your performance is transformed from a thinking process to a more automatic one, much like riding a bike. In other words, you have gained and stored knowledge and a feel for whatever it is that you have learned for future use.

As your left side of the brain identifies the steps that are necessary to perform well, whether through instruction, practice or note-taking, the thinking needed to perform these functions can then give way to just doing. I refer to this process as having a feel for the game.

Technical training and the mental side of the game comprise the game of golf or any sport for that matter.

Interestingly, as you learn to deal with the mental side of a game, you can also learn to apply those same principles to managing your life.

It is important to realize that your mind is just that, YOUR MIND. It doesn't belong to the last bad shot or the person with whom you're competing with in match play or even to the designer who built the course. It is you.

The more effectively you use your mind, the more progress you can make and the more enjoyable your experience can become. Learning how to train your mind to have thoughts and feelings that provide the greatest advantage possible is as important as any other training that you might receive. Purchasing new equipment as the answer to more proficient play is enjoyable and exciting but keeps in mind that the game was originally played with a few hickory sticks. New equipment can help you feel better and along with modern technology can have a positive influence on both the technical and mental side of your game. But equipment alone isn't going to change how you think, feel and strike the ball with accuracy.

There is nothing magical about learning how to play the game of golf. Technically, it is a matter of learning what your body needs to do to perform or produce good golf shots. Many body parts need to be coordinated to make proper contact with the ball. However, you can make the game more difficult by paying too much attention to unimportant, piecemeal information. When watching the pros, you can tell whether they are in their zone or whether they are preoccupied with a new grip or swing.

29

A good example that comes to mind is when my two young sons learned how to play the game of golf. Both of them were playing hockey at the time and, of course, wanted to develop a slap shot like the pros. When I taught them the proper grip and stance over the ball, I said, "Now hit it!" On the first try, they hit a good shot and now, as adults, they have a very solid game.

I attribute their success during that first lesson to the body movement they learned in practicing the slap shot in hockey, which they then carried over into the game of golf. This is what is meant by a positive carryover effect.

Another example of a problem that might arise is when a golfer accepts a pro's advice as gospel without interpreting it in a manner that makes the pro's advice his/her experience. You must do your own research and although the instruction you receive may be helpful, using someone else's words usually doesn't enable you to fully understand what works best for you.

One of my clients was very interested in having his fourteen year old son play well in his town's golf league. He felt that his son had great potential and wanted him to improve so he decided to give him some golf lessons. The young man's score increased instead of decreasing because his natural swing became too technical and he stopped having fun playing the golf. The boy's enthusiasm dwindled and he ultimately decided to give up golf. This is a good example of taking another person's advice literally without bringing that advice into your own experience.

The problem was probably neither the pro's advice nor the instruction. What happened was that the youngster never took that instruction and processed it until it became his own method. Granted, most changes are initially uncomfortable but should that discomfort continue for a long time, it is doubtful that the approach will ever become an essential part of the golfer's useable knowledge. The lessons are in the pro's words, concepts and instructions. You must then put those lessons into your own language so that they become your experience. No amount of practice will change this process. Instead the result will probably become a disjointed series of steps instead of a fluid, satisfying performance.

Developing a natural movement is one of the keys to playing the game of golf well.

Forming Good Golfing Habits

Although all of the technical elements of the golf are important to learn and implement, if they haven't become a natural part of your experience, they are just that - technical elements. In order to control your body to experience a good shot, it is first necessary to learn to use your mind to form your thoughts. I propose that in order to form good golfing habits and shoot well you first need to:

1) Gain a basic understanding of the fundamentals of the game of golf,
2) Learn to use both your mind and body to execute various shots,
3) Develop and maintain a solid practice regimen,
4) Develop a feel for your performance while playing.

Now, let's take a closer look at each one of these points.

Understanding the fundamentals of the game:

The fundamentals of the game refer to a combination of learning the rules and regulations that govern etiquette and play as well as the basic technical aspects necessary for effective club selection. I highly recommend that you purchase a copy of the Rules of Golf and read it carefully to have a positive impact on the mental side of your game.

Proper procedures and etiquette are an essential part of the game of golf. In addition, you need to make your own adjustments to your game. You need to get a feel for the grip, stance, swing, etc. in order for these technical aspects to become part of your knowledge base so that you can repeat them on a consistent basis.

Your instructor should always ask how his recommendation feels to you. Your job is to determine how you feel and decide what works best for you.

Training your mind and body to execute shots:

Learning to swing a club is clearly not simply a physical exercise. The mind and body need to constantly communicate and send messages back and forth to each other so that it ultimately becomes an automatic process. This takes time, consistent and repetitive practice and a good deal of patience. Learning the game is not like going to McDonald's and grabbing a quick hamburger. Your body is a very complicated and involved system of tendons, muscles, etc. that is accustomed to performing in a certain manner. However, the game of golf demands that the body perform in ways that are foreign to what it usually does.

Furthermore, the game is one of intense precision requiring the re-training of both your gross and fine motor skills in order to perform the required elements. The more that you use your mind to achieve a specific goal, like mastering a shot with a particular golf club, the more capable you will be to accomplish a similar result with other aspects of the game. Taking notes on your progress for reviewing at a later time can help you perform in a consistent manner. One of the more advanced techniques used by instructors is to take a video of a golfer's swing, which further demonstrates the need for gaining a feel for the game. Once again, you need to find out what works best for you.

Developing and maintaining a solid practice regimen:

I have always said that the one lesson that the game of golf teaches is humility. Not unusually, once you work on one part of your game to achieve a goal or correct a problem, there will always be another part that needs attention to take its place. That truth holds up for amateurs and professionals alike. However, if you're going to take the game seriously and want to progress, it is vital that you develop and maintain a solid practice regimen. Going to the range just to hit balls will rarely improve your game. However, going to hit balls for the purpose of correcting a problem or executing a new shot usually produces an improvement.

Having a plan in golf, as in life, is worthy of note. Prior to playing a round, some form of warm-up should take place to reacquaint you with the technical parts of the game. As with anything else, we all tend to get rusty after a layover between rounds and even if we play daily, the warm-up fundamentally gets us into the groove of our game instead of taking two or three holes to accomplish that result.

Many golfers have a ritual that they follow during their practice regimen. Some golfers bring the notes that they have written while playing rounds or after practice sessions to remind them of their experiences. This could range from the use of their driver to their putting routine. However, your practice regimen should not be random. It should involve a methodical process that allows you to touch upon parts of your game that you want to work on.

You might decide to invent little games while practicing to improve your play as well as to sharpen the mental side of your game. I have devoted a section of this book to games that you might try to achieve these results. It is in the section entitled *"Playing games with the game."*

The regimen you choose should be specifically aimed at helping you gain a greater sense of confidence, which you can take with you when you play a round.

Essentially, the purpose of practicing is to train or retrain your body and mind to perform in a manner that brings about improvement. It is the manner in which you train your mind, body and emotions to decipher what not only what works best but also what feels most comfortable.

In your practice sessions you should first picture what you want to achieve in your mind. This will help you accomplish your goals and make whatever changes you are working on a permanent part of your golf game. This does not mean that what you learn through practice is written in stone. The game of golf requires that you work on swing fundamentals whenever you decide that an improvement is required. It is all a matter of adjusting your swing to reach your next performance plateau.

A good example of this is the changes that you need to make as your body undergoes normal changes associated with aging. Your body's flexibility lessens with age and you must adapt to that change, whether in golf or in your daily routine. In any event, it is an on-going process, never ends. To believe that you have finally got it all together is folly.

Developing a feel for your performance while playing:

Proper equipment and technical training are very important in order to play golf well. However, these facets taken by themselves will usually not produce better or consistent play. Consistent play comes from the feel for the game that you can develop through the mental side of golf. Your feeling comes from your recollection of what you have previously experienced. For some people, it takes the form of note-taking or simply remembering how a particular club felt while previously being swung.

The formula is simple. Keep track of what you do and how you feel when you do it. The most effective way of doing this is to take both written and mental notes but some people only take the time to make mental notes. It's a simple matter of cause and effect. "When I do this, I feel like that" or "When I feel like this, I usually do that." It goes both ways and the more aware you can be, the more you can get that feel, maintain focus and stay in your zone. If you realize that when you are feeling a certain way you make a poor shot, you can challenge yourself to remember that you did to produce the feeling that you experience from a good shot. This speaks to the power of the mental side of the game of golf. The more you do what is required to have positive thoughts, the more you will think, feel and act to have a great game of golf.

I remember playing golf as a single and being placed with a man in his mid-70's. He played six days a week and walked the 6,800 yard course with some difficulty because he was severely bowlegged and had a hip condition, both of which limited his body movements. He had an awful swing but he consistently parred the course. Over time, he learned to compensate and adapt his swing to compensate for his physical handicap. This clearly illustrates that there is not just one swing that works. His attitude was very positive. He enjoyed his game and exuded confidence.

At times I found myself watching him play instead of attending to my own game because of his phenomenal consistency. He loved the game and talked freely about his experiences. He was a pleasure to meet and he was a good golfing partner.

Although this book is not focused on the technical aspects of the game or on physical training, this example clearly demonstrates how people can use their mind to accept physical handicaps and at the same time establish high expectations for success. I am sure that no one taught him how to adapt his golf swing. Instead, he made a natural change because of his love of the game and because he recognized his strengths and limitations. Essentially, the skill he acquired involved emotional, physical and intellectual challenges.

The lessons I learned from this handicapped golfer were to accept my less than perfect golf swing, relax and enjoy the game of golf. You can use your mind to figure out how to compensate to get almost any job done. You can also learn to trust your instincts. I have included a few references to some technical aspects of the game of golf to enforce principles of the mental side of golf.

Developing
A Strategy

Recently, when asked about his new driver at the 2006 Buick Open, Tiger Woods exclaimed that the driver was just fine but what was more important was the person holding the club. Interestingly, several of his drives went to the right and into the rough. As a result, he needed to hit an innovative second shot to reach the green. Did Tiger have a mind set operating? Probably he did. Ultimately, he won the tournament by one stroke after two exciting sudden death playoff holes.

Tiger Woods has a remarkable ability to rebound when his back is up against the wall. This takes tremendous self-discipline and extensive physical and mental training. Even though he may get frustrated and even angry at times, he is usually able to rebound, resume focus and return to his zone. I followed him while attending the Rochester PGA Tournament a few years ago. His ability to rebound was apparent throughout the tournament. He may not win every tournament but his ability to adapt to almost any situation provides a great deal of excitement for his fans.

In Tiger's early years in the PGA, he tended to place as much emphasis on the mental side of the game as he did on the technical and physical elements. He certainly developed himself physically to give him the endurance necessary to achieve his boundless potential. When Tiger was younger, I recall how he would seem to get upset when cameras clicked on the sidelines while he putted or when people made noise while he was driving the ball. He would pull back, appear angry and glare at the spectator who caused the distraction.

One of the stories concerns the time when Tiger asked his father to help him overcome distractions. Just before Tiger was ready to putt, his father jiggled his keys to create an annoying distraction. Learning to overcome this distraction enabled Tiger to teach himself to overcome any distraction.

I'm sure there were many other training methods that Tiger used to sharpen his skills by using his mind, body and emotions to enable him to stay in his zone. Developing a strategy for yourself is as important for the amateur as it is for the professional if you want to progress in your game. It would be a good idea if you could consciously develop new ways of training yourself to become more self-disciplined as well. It may not be easy but the outcome will certainly be satisfying and extremely useful in dealing with both the game of golf as well as life in general.

Jack Nicklaus, who is probably recognized as one of golf's most proficient thinkers and strategists had this to say:

"Golf calls for two interrelated but distinct skills. One is the ability to strike the ball, to physically play the shots. The other is the ability to observe, evaluate, plan and think your way around the golf course, to play strategically and tactically - in short, to score. No matter how good you become at the first, you'll never be a successful golfer if you are not equally good at the second."

This statement is a clear and definitive way of understanding the importance of the mental side of the game of golf. Gaining a sense of satisfaction from your golf game is not only derived from striking the ball but striking it and landing it strategically in an area that will afford a good, effective subsequent shot in order to score well. There is a great deal of emphasis placed on power golf. However, it seems to me that power golf can only be effectively practiced until a golfer is able to develop a strategy for playing the game. Distance does not necessarily insure accuracy.

This kind of thinking places the game into our hands and not into the occasional lucky chance shot that keeps you coming back. This kind of thinking will allow consistency in your game that you can count on in future rounds. The lie of the ball, the choice of the club, the length of the backswing, the area into which you want to place the ball, the anticipation of the next shot...all of these factors play into the thinking and strategy that you can bring to your game.

A good friend of mine likens the game of golf to a game of chess. Instead of focusing on the score or the mechanics of the game, he maintains that golfers should be more aware of the layout of the course. He contends that the strategy behind the game, for both beginners and professionals, should deal with beating the course architect. Golf course architects trick players with obstacles and mirages that tend to cause golfers to take risks that are beyond their current ability. For example, there might be long distances that appear short or unseen water hazards that block the entrance to a green. Another example is that although it might appear that a wood should be the club of choice off a tee, you might be better off using an iron to hit short of water hazard leaving a safe and high probability chip to the green.

My friend also approaches his game with a different perceptual outlook as well as how he might play a course.

He always acquaints himself with the course design before playing. A commentator at the 2006 Master's Tournament, while commenting on the participants' progress, said, "I am afraid that the course has won this round." The commentator's remark supports my friend's approach.

When we develop the strategy of beating the course, the competitive aspects take on a different sense. Essentially, play becomes a mind game where you can have some fun indulging in outsmarting the architect's attempts to entice you to take too many or too few risks. Andre Agassi, the tennis player, once did a TV commercial that claimed perception is everything. Perception is everything but it is not only a matter of what we see but of how we see it.

When you choose a particular club to make a shot, your choice is based on your prior experience. You remember how you approached this shot in the past and how it felt. You also take a moment to remember and focus on what you were thinking and feeling. There was probably a feeling of confidence that you would make the shot.

You might remember taking a lesson on how to use that club more effectively and how you were able to reformulate what the instructor was saying into your own words. And you might also recall the feeling that you had once you had accomplished striking the ball and sending it to the desired location. These are all your thoughts and feelings. You can recall and use them whenever you wish. Retrieving prior thoughts and feelings is truly an effective strategy.

Now, let's look at the flip side of the positive example. What if the last time you used a club, you hit a poor shot. You can still employ a positive thinking strategy. Remember what you were thinking of and how you felt the last time you were disappointed. Try recalling those thoughts and feelings as clearly and precisely as possible. Being aware of prior negative thoughts is a totally different situation. You can use your mind to move away from those negative thoughts and create new thoughts and feelings. Of course, you must also recall swing fundamentals. Take a little bit of time to imagine a correct swing and then execute your swing in a positive manner. Learn how to rid your mind of negative experiences as you recall swing fundamentals and execute each shot knowing that you will succeed.

You don't have to feel something that will further complicate your problem. You can always feel confident and focused on the next shot that is within your ability to execute. Don't rush your thoughts. No one else needs to know what you're doing. That's it! Notice how positive your thinking is and how good this feels. Take a practice swing with these thoughts and feelings. It feels good doesn't it? Now, address the ball, take your time and swing with the confidence that the ball will jump off the face of the club and land where you want it to go. This type of confidence will usually produce a positive result. With time, this practice and attitude will work consistently.

There is something about a score that not only makes some golfers tense and jittery, but also prevents them from relaxing. All of this results in a less than desirable effect. In golf jargon, it's called the yips. Trying to kill the ball frequently reduces distance just as an overly competitive attitude can increase your score. Although scoring is a necessary part of the game it should never more important than remaining focused, implementing your strategic plan and staying in your zone.

The more relaxed and focused you are as you approach a round of golf, the more effectively you will be able to play.

This does not only refer to relaxing your mind and body. You need to also place emphasis on developing a strategy for playing the game to minimize tension, improve play and help you enjoy the game. This same principle can be applied to managing your life. Learning how to accomplish this will make a big difference in your golf game as well as in your life.

And now, I want to introduce you to a strategy exercise so that you can see in detail how you might approach any course that you might play. If you play only one course, you can apply the strategic elements to every hole on the course. I believe that if you are sincerely dedicated to using this approach, you will shave strokes off of your game in a relatively short period of time. Let's first examine what the specific purposes are for developing a strategy.

PURPOSES OF A STRATEGY EXERCISE

• A strategy allows us to approach a problem in a systematic and logical manner;
• A strategy must be based in HONESTY, A POSITIVE ATTITUDE, REASONABLE EXPECTATIONS and A WILLINGNESS TO ACCEPT CHANGES IN ORDER TO SUCCEED;
• A strategy includes being able to break down complex problems into smaller "pieces" in order to change the whole picture;
• Vision each picture of each shot while remembering the thoughts and feelings of previous shots, practice sessions;
• Off any and all tees, describe how you feel taking the shot and then doffing it into the water/rough/ sand trap, etc.;

43

- The goal is to achieve your PERSONAL BEST for each shot you play;
- Bring a SENSE OF HONESTY and REALISTIC EXPECTATIONS in order to determine effectiveness, changes in approaching each shot, etc.;
- Envisioning each shot, club, swing, where ball's going to land comes from previous experiences with all of them IN PLAY AND PRACTICE SESSIONS;
- Not just THINKING of every swing but what it FELT LIKE WHEN YOU WERE SUCCESSFUL;
- You won't really be able to remember everything unless you write it down since the mind's recall ability needs stimulation.

For your information, you can go to the internet and do a Google search for whichever course for which you would like to develop a STRATEGIC PLAN. Many courses are able to be found together with a layout and description of each hole. That having been said, there are some courses that are not represented in this manner and your going to the course to get descriptive information would be your next best bet or send for that information should you be traveling to the course out of town.

For demonstration purposes, I have chosen the 6th hole on my home course, Bobcat Trail in North Port, Florida. I've chosen this hole because in playing the course, it affords me more trouble than satisfaction. It is the longest hole on the course and the hazards that border it truly tests my ability to hit a straight, accurately placed shot in order to par the hole.

Before sending you to **TABLE 1** I want to say that I've usually bogeyed or double bogeyed this hole. In my last attempt, though, I employed the strategy which will be defined in **TABLE 2**. Instead of using a driver off the tee, I decided to use my three wood in order to gain a greater sense of accuracy instead of going for distance and running the risk of shooting into a hazard. I focused on each of my shots using the visualization techniques described in a latter section of this book. In effect, it worked. Each shot took on a very different perspective both in terms of my choice of clubs as well as my technical form. I was much more aware of my play, my sense of focus and staying in my zone which enabled me to par the hole. I was elated and I believe that you will be as well once you develop your own strategy for your golf game.

TABLE 1 on the following two pages contains an overall description of the course, the Men's and Women's yardage from the 6th tee, the par for the hole and a section asking that you place your most realistic score ONLY UPON COMPLETING YOUR STRATEGIC PLAN FOR THIS HOLE.. Descriptions of the fairway leading to the green are added. Then, you are asked to provide your own THOUGHTS and FEELINGS about playing the hole for each shot taken including your putts.

TABLE 1

BOBCAT TRAIL HOLE NO. 6

Bobcat Trail Golf Club plays 6748 yards, par 71 from the tips and is the only Golf Digest rated 4½ star golf course in Sarasota County. Designed by Canadian Open Champion and PGA Champion, Bob Tway, and architect Lee Singletary, "The Cat" is a rewarding challenge for players of all skill levels.

Every hole at Bobcat Trail is a distinctive "risk-reward" design and any one of the 18 could be considered the signature hole. The keys to scoring on "The Cat" are well placed drives on the wide rolling fairways, accurate irons to the proper "shelf" and imagination and steady nerves on and around the large, undulating and well-bunkered greens.

No. 6
Distance: 532 Yards (Men's Green)
            428 Yards (Women's Red)
Par: 5
Score: _____ Insert your most realistic score after you complete your plan for the 6th hole.

The 6th hole is one of the most difficult holes on "The Cat." It is the longest hole on the course. The 6th hole rewards accurate play up the middle of the fairway and an accurate approach shot over the hazard that protects a large undulating green that has three shelves.

The initial fairway has a number of slopes on both the right and left. There is a water hazard on the entire right length of the fairway and rough, cart path and homes on the left length of the fairway. Shots such as sliced, pushed, pulled, duck hooked shots cause the loss of one or more strokes.

The initial fairway narrows just where long drives are supposed to land.

The second fairway is protected on the right by rough and a well placed sand trap (medium consistency) and several sand traps at the far left center of the fairway to penalize the errant shots of long hitters. There is another water hazard just over the cart path at the far end of the second fairway.

The approach shot to the green is a dogleg right over a hazard. The slightly elevated green has three shelves and is protected by two sand traps (medium sand) on the far right and banks and rough around the entire green.

Add your own descriptive (thoughts & feelings) comments about the 6th hole below:

_____

_____

_____

1st Shot_____

_____

2nd Shot_____

_____

3rd Shot_____

_____

Putts_____

_____

Add your own comments about your most realistic score below and/or on reverse side:

_____

_____

_____

Add your own comments about "The Mental Side of Golf" below and/or on reverse side:

_____

_____

_____

TABLE 2 is essentially the same as **TABLE 1** except it contains my completion of the required information in order to complete my strategic plan for the hole. I completed it with the help (and criticism) of my good friend, Roy, who designed this Strategic Plan. His insistence on my honesty and what my clear expectations were helped me to focus even more specifically on my play which I tended to take for granted and to which I seldom had paid much attention. It was a very interesting and revealing exercise in which I would invite all readers to engage so that your awareness of developing a strategy can become more astute as well.

TABLE 2

Bobcat Trail Golf Club plays 6748 yards, par 71 from the tips and is the only Golf Digest rated 4½ star golf course in Sarasota County. Designed by Canadian Open Champion and PGA Champion, Bob Tway, and architect Lee Singletary, **"The Cat"** is a rewarding challenge for players of all skill levels.

Every hole at **Bobcat Trail** is a distinctive "risk-reward" design and any one of the 18 could be considered the signature hole. The keys to scoring on **"The Cat"** are well placed drives on the wide rolling fairways, accurate irons to the proper "shelf" and imagination and steady nerves on and around the large, undulating and well-bunkered greens.

No. 6
Distance: 532 Yards (Men's Green)
            428 Yards (Women's Red)
Par: 5
Score: 6

The 6th hole is one of the most difficult holes on **"The Cat."** It is the longest hole on the course. The 6th hole rewards accurate play up the middle of the fairway and an accurate approach shot over the hazard that protects a large undulating green that has three shelves.

The initial fairway has a number of slopes on both the right and left. There is a water hazard on the entire right length of the fairway and rough, cart path and homes on the left length of the fairway. Shots such as sliced, pushed, pulled, duck hooked shots cause the loss of one or more strokes.

The initial fairway narrows just where long drives are supposed to land.

The second fairway is protected on the right by rough and a well placed sand trap (medium consistency) and several sand traps at the far left center of the fairway to penalize the errant shots of long hitters. There is another water hazard just over the cart path at the far end of the second fairway.

The approach shot to the green is a dogleg right over a hazard. The slightly elevated green has three shelves and is protected by two sand traps (medium sand) on the far right and banks and rough around the entire green.

Add your own descriptive comments about the 6th hole below: *This hole is my nemesis. No. 6 appears much longer than it really is. I usually played this hole too long. I was always tense when I stood on the tee and usually sprayed my drives.*

1st Shot *3-Wood Concentrate on easy swing with a light grip and my follow-through. Envision my prior 3-Wood shot. The ball will be in the middle of the fairway about 200 yards from the tee.*

2nd Shot *4-Iron to center of the fairway. Focus is on smooth takeaway. Envision top of backswing. Ball will be center left about 170 yards from the green (plays like 135 yards).*

3rd Shot *7-Iron or 8-Iron depending on distance. Ball position is 1 width right of center stance. Concentrate on slow takeaway for at least 2 feet, a 75% backswing and hitting down and through the ball. Ball will be on the green about 20' from the pin.*

Putts *Three putts for a bogey 6. I usually score a double bogey or higher on this hole because I have always hit a driver and tried to reach this green in regulation. I expect* *this plan to enable me to par this hole 30% of the time. A key factor for me is to play this hole as if I am playing in a tournament.*

Add your own comments about "The Mental Side of Golf" below: *I didn't know that there was this much to the mental side of golf. I must put my expectations into a more practical perspective. I will complete my strategic plan for "The Cat." I will let Charlie know about my experience.*

TABLE 3 is simply a prototype of the previous two tables which you can copy and use to develop a strategic strategy for all of the holes on the course of your choice. The process is challenging but enjoyable. I can all but guarantee that you will shave strokes off of your game if you conscientiously apply this strategy to your game. Remember though, before you play a course that is new to you, get to the course early and along with going to the practice range to work on some of your weak points **(SEE SECTION ON "FORMING GOOD GOLFING HABITS")** you should also spend some time looking over the course layout and determine your strategy accordingly. Take some notes. If you are playing in a tournament and are able to play a practice round, or walk the course, take copious notes to which you can refer in the course of playing a tournament round. You will find that there will be a payoff at the end of the round in terms of better, more focused and confident play.

TABLE 3

GOLF COURSE NAME & HOLE NUMBER

COURSE DESCRIPTION:

_____
_____
_____

DESCRIPTION OF DESIRED HOLE:

_____
_____
_____

    Hole No.
    Distance: Yards (Men's Green)
              Yards (Women's Red)
    Hole Par:
    Score:__   Insert your most realistic score after you complete your plan for this hole.

Specific description of your desired hole:

_____
_____
_____

Add your own descriptive comments about this hole below:

_____

_____

_____

1st Shot:

_____

_____

2nd Shot:

_____

_____

3rd Shot:

_____

_____

4th Shot:

_____

_____

Putts:_____

_____

Add your own descriptive (thoughts & feelings) comments about this hole below:

_____

_____

_____

Add your own comments about your most realistic score below:

_____

_____

_____

Add your own comments about "The Mental Side of Golf" below:

_____

_____

_____

Tournament Preparation
(Maintaining Focus in Competition)

For the average golfer, golf is a game but for professionals it is also an exciting competitive sport for which one's talents are rewarded. Throughout this book, I recommend that little attention should be paid to your score. That would still hold up for those not involved in competitive play. But in a way, it should not be a preoccupation for those in tournament play either. Here is my reasoning.

Competition is an essential part of all sports. Everyone likes to win. My concern is about how you compete. In golf, competition has to do with attaining a low score. The other person's mistakes might better your chances but you can't be preoccupied with these issues and maintain focus on your own game at the same time. Competition comes from an external force. It is based on the need to defeat your opponents with the focus being on the other golfers. And so, instead of the focus being on yourself and your game, it is on your opponent. Some tournament golfers become so preoccupied with their competitors' scores that they don't pay attention to their own game plan.

An interesting interchange recently took place between Arnold Palmer and Jack Nicklaus during an interview conducted by Jim Nance on CBS TV at the 2006 Memorial Golf Tournament in Dublin, Ohio. A couple of the points that they made struck me as being illustrative of the need to focus on your own game during competition.

Arnold and Jack were talking about their early years of

playing against each other and the degree of competition that existed between them. Palmer said that they were both well aware of the rules of tournament play. However, instead of focusing on the tournament itself, they focused on defeating each other, and neither of them won the tournament.

At a different tournament, Palmer thought he had better concentrate on his own game instead of competing with Nicklaus. He won that tournament and defeated Jack. Earlier in his career, when Nicklaus was very young and just beginning tournament play, he was paired with Arnold Palmer. He was struggling to defeat Palmer and his game was suffering as a result. On one of the holes, Palmer took him aside and advised him to relax and play his game so that he might at least come in second instead of finishing further down the leader board.

These examples concern the pressure of tournament play but also to show that much of the pressure comes from a false view of competition. If you really think about it, Palmer's advice was just a matter of simple logic, which Nicklaus applied and successfully accomplished.

The example of two of the greatest golfers of our time talking about some of the mental errors that they committed is intended to help you understand that even accomplished players can lose perspective and focus during the game of golf. The element of competition can do that to anyone. You can get so caught up in the need to win, whether in a tournament, match play or a friendly competitive game that your primary purpose of playing the game can get lost in the shuffle.

Your primary purpose should be to bring all of your talents to bear during a round so that, despite a loss, you can look back and say that you were satisfied with your performance despite the mistakes that you may have made along the way. It is all about being able to recognize when you have played to the best of your ability.

On any given day, a golfer could win or lose a tournament. There are many PGA and LPGA tournaments where unknowns have risen to the occasion and won tournaments despite the fact that the ranking golfers were being followed by their many fans as well as the press. This tells me that talent is beginning to become distributed over the field of players in the professional ranks. Many fans want the old favorites to win but I find it refreshing that young players have developed the focus and ability to stay in their zone, despite the tremendous stress and pressure that come from playing against he world's top ranked players.

There is always room for excellence in any endeavor. New records are always being achieved in all sports.

This really adds much excitement to watching sports. I look upon this as a testimony of how people can use their minds and physical abilities to conquer seemingly insurmountable obstacles.

However, the mental side of golf can sometimes fail the best golfers. In the 2006 LPGA Jamie Farr Owens Corning Classic, there were a number of high ranked golfers, who were followed by the press in anticipation of the winner being among them. Julie Inkstrom, Anika Sorenstam, Se Ri Pak and Mi Hyun Kim were the favorites.

In addition, Natalie Gublis and Paula Creamer, two young contenders who had never won a major tournament, seemed to be holding their own.

As the tournament progressed, all of the well known

golfers except for Mi Kim Hyun gradually fell back. Paula Creamer had difficulty keeping her drives on the fairway as well as her putting stroke. Mi Hyun Kim and Natalie Gublis were tied for the lead at the finish. The announcers repeatedly talked about how poised Natalie Gublis was and that this could be a win for a relatively unknown golfer.

Mi Hyun Kim and Natalie Gublis began their sudden death playoff on the 18th hole. Both golfers played very well. They hit almost identical shots from tee to green and putted well, resulting in a second playoff hole on the 17th. Once again, the same neck and neck play occurred necessitating an exciting third playoff hole back on the 18th. Prior to the first sudden death hole, I watched the two leaders very carefully. Natalie Gublis, a beautiful young lady was walking proudly, smiling at the fans and cameras and gleefully chatting with her caddy between shots.

It was obvious that she had a huge following and had been accustomed to posing for magazines and calendars. Her opponent later commented on how large a following Gulbis had to the extent that they were cheering for her as they walked the course between shots. However, Mi Hyun Kim seemed to be walking with a sense of purpose. I leaned over and told my wife, Barbara, that Mi Hyun Kim appeared to have her game face on and I predicted that she would win the tournament.

It came down to the last putt on the third playoff hole. As the camera focused on Natalie Gublis, I noticed a brief look of doubt on her face as she stared down a 12 foot putt. After Mi Hyun Kim sunk her 18 foot putt, Natalie Gublis missed her twelve foot putt. Mi Hyun Kim won the tournament. My sense was that Natalie Gublis lost her focus and succumbed to the moment of glory.

Later Natalie Gublis said that prior to her last putt, she

felt that she was a shoe-in to win the tournament. I think that everyone in the gallery expected the popular Gulbis to defeat Kim. However, popularity doesn't win tournaments; a golfer's overall focus on each shot and the ability to remain in his/her zone are the key factors for success.

What does this mean for the average, non-professional golfer? It means that the mental side of golf is as important as the physical and mechanical side of golf. You may not acquire fame or break records in your golf play but you can always work to achieve your potential. The only limitation that you place on yourself is doubt of your ability to improve. It isn't your competitor or tournament pressure or your technical ability that limits you. Granted, on any given day you may do poorly but that does not need to become the rule unless you get down on yourself and believe that poor play is the best you can do. My guess is that Mi Hyun Kim believed in herself despite the pressure of the moment stemming from her opponent's popularity.

Probably the best training that you can accomplish is living your life on a daily basis. There are many things that you can do to begin to train yourself to look beyond the present.

The three keys to personal happiness are:

1. To always have something to look forward to,
2. To develop and maintain a sense of humor, and
3. To bring as much love into your life as is possible.

It may sound too simple, but try practicing these three keys over the period of at least a week and see what happens in your personal life as well as in your golf game.

Paying attention to these three keys for any part of your life will carryover into your golf game as well. That is a promise.

That is why the real challenge of golf comes from you. Instead of feeling defeated and reaching the depths of despair, while questioning whether or not you should continue playing the game after a poor round, you should form a positive mind set that causes you to do better the next time. Reach for the heights. When you think of what you have already accomplished in your life, at times against stiff odds and after making persistent attempts, you should trust your experience and move positively to accomplish your goals. You can't win all the time and you are not meant to, nor is anyone else for that matter. Maybe losing or having a bad game is nature's way of helping us to appreciate winning or just playing a good round of golf. It is all a matter of your perspective, being kind to yourself, being patient and realizing that golf is not a game of perfect.

In the 2006 Player's Open, Tiger Woods was interviewed and asked how he was able to maintain his focus while his father and best friend was very ill on the west coast. He thought for a moment and said that he had just returned from visiting him in order to help bolster his spirits. He felt that he had done everything he could. It appeared that he was attempting to manage the effects of his concern for his father's health to the extent possible in order to play that particular match. He didn't try to make his sad thoughts and feelings go away. Instead, he was managing them.

I find some people's perception of Woods (and sometimes of themselves) to be very unfair. People tend to view Tiger as being superhuman and expect him to perform accordingly. His humanity was clearly demonstrated when he won the 2006 British Open. When his final putt went into the hole, Tiger fell into his caddy's arms and sobbed uncontrollably as he thought about the loss of his father. Sometimes our expectations of ourselves tend to exceed what we can actually do as well.

This type of perspective takes a great deal of self-discipline, which can only be developed over time. There are always issues, problems or concerns that may interfere with playing the game of golf, so this example doesn't just hold true for Tiger Woods but for all of us. Being able to maintain focus, despite whatever our interruptive thoughts might be, takes a great deal of inner strength and self-discipline.

Going to the practice range can help train your mind to achieve that sense of self discipline. Although you probably don't spend as much time practicing as professionals do, the time spent should have a specific purpose. That sense of purpose and how to develop focus is gained from how we approach our practice sessions. Our mind can rise above the interruptions that are common in all of our lives but if we are more accustomed to letting those thoughts take us over, then, of course, we will be at their mercy while on the golf course. The more we can do to discipline ourselves, the greater the possibility that we can block them out, at least while we are focusing on our game. Of course, another key factor that needs mentioning is to take care of whatever needs attention in your personal life so that those feelings and thoughts won't interfere with your golf game.

We might learn something from what professionals take away from their practice sessions. What might a professional golfer go through to prepare for a tournament or even a casual round? What value will practicing have in developing your mental side of the game of golf?

Professional golfers generally go through a regimen that prepares them for tournament play. Each golfer may have a different order or may place a different emphasis on their regimen but there are essential similarities. Of course, the practice sessions are designed to work on either developing new shots or correcting problems that they might have with their grip, swing, stance, tempo, pace, etc. Professional golfers spend hours on the practice range with this exhausting work. Sometimes they are guided by their personal golf instructor/coach.

There may be a great deal of trial and error attempts made to develop a feel for their progress. To the extent possible, they work at making whatever changes they are working on as comfortable as possible so that the lessons learned can be more easily applied to their actual play. The more they practice a change of routine, let's say with a particular club, the more comfortable they become, which leads to being able to execute like shots instinctively. Each golfer must make his/her own determination of the comfort they must have to instinctively accomplish each shot during actual tournament play.

The test for what he/she has accomplished on the practice range is accomplished during their practice rounds. Playing the course that hosts the tournament just before the actual tournament is essential to gain a sense of the course's layout and specific site factors that they are likely to encounter at each hole.

Usually, golfers and their caddies take copious notes on each hole to document how each hole might best be played from multiple locations. These notes might include trouble spots that they experience during practice rounds.

Each practice session usually exceeds the eighteen holes that non-professionals are accustomed to playing, which can make it very tiring work. Their practice rounds are systematic and purposeful to enable the golfers and their caddies to experience a variety of circumstances that they might possibly experience during the tournament. Love of the game and the competitive challenge compensates for all of this hard work.

Some of their notes might describe experiencing the yips before specific shots. Also, they might have hired a professional, who coaches them on their mental approach. Today, many of the touring professionals are working with mental coaches to improve this important aspect of their game. Sometimes the mental coach will accompany the golfer to tournaments or might be available for phone consultations prior to and following each round.

This mental coach works with the golfer on developing strategies that he/she might use during the tournament to help them maintain their focus and stay in their zone. The mental coach might suggest some relaxation techniques or find ways to help the golfer deal with his/her anxiety caused by the immediate pressure of tournament play. The goal is to correct emerging problems before they become a slump, from which recovery is impossible.

An ounce of prevention is always worth more than a pound of cure.

In summary, the preparation that professionals go through is extensive and painstaking so that they are able to achieve their potential during tournament play. I wouldn't expect the average golfer to go through all of those steps but it is important, even in a friendly game, that some preparation be accomplished if the golfer wants to progress. The training methods that I suggest that every golfer perform are good examples of the methods that professional golfers use.

9

The Caddie's Role

In 1997, Dennis Cone formed the Professional Caddie Association. He said, "If you never played with a caddie, you've never really played the game." He went on to say, "In its purest form, golf is all about the walk, visualizing the shot, getting the focus. You have someone to assist you so that your mind is in that mode without all the running around and conversation. It's not just reading the green, it's the experience overall. A good caddie takes strokes off your game."

I found this in an article while I was traveling on a plane. Certainly, caddies play an important role in the preparation that golfers go through for a tournament. I refer to a good caddie as the golfer's alter ego because of the additional perspective they bring to each shot and situation. There is an old saying, "When two people think alike, there's not much thinking going on." Caddies bring that second opinion to bear that can often make the difference between success and failure.

I am sure that Mr. Cone is right but nevertheless, most golfers have never and probably will never experience the benefit of playing golf with a caddie. However, it is important that all of the functions that a caddie can offer a golfer become part of every golfer's approach to the game. This is why I suggest that every golfer go through a training exercise to establish the mind set that will allow him/her to perform these functions for themselves. Mastering these training techniques can't take the place of a good caddie, but mental training can become an important part of everyone's plan to improve their game.

Developing the Mental Side of Your Game

In order to develop the mental side of your game, your practicing regimen should achieve the following:

1. Develop a sense of self-discipline that will carry over both into your play and personal life as well.
2. Practice set routines in order to develop a systematic practice schedule which can lead to developing a strategy for play.
3. Clear your mind of carryover effects; this means the distracting issues, thoughts and feelings that interfere with maintaining focus and staying in your zone.
4. Develop a relaxed, confident attitude that will carry over into competition or even into a casual round.
5. Develop an unconscious feel for everything you have accomplished during practice so that you can better carry that feeling over into your game in order to stay in your zone.

Developing a sense of self-discipline that will carry over into your golf game and personal life

Golf is a game of precision that requires golfers to develop a disciplined approach to step-wise improvement. Everyone who continues to play the game of golf wants to improve his/her performance. Becoming frustrated when you make a poor shot is a clear indication that you want to improve. If the primary purpose of your practice sessions is to train yourself to become more disciplined, the chances of improving your game will be greater. Use notes from your last round to remind you of what you previously felt. Use your imagination aided by your notes to re-play each shot in your mind.

Hit various shots from different positions in a sand trap that is in front of a green to develop your feeling for the mechanics that produce shots that stop within 10 feet of the pin. Do the same thing with chipping from different positions on the apron of a green. As you memorize the feeling of making good shots, you will be disciplining yourself. Developing a disciplined practice regimen that enables you to also work on the mental side of your game is very important for lasting improvement. Establishing stepwise mental and mechanical goals for the improvement of each shot helps you establish priorities.

Invent games that place obstacles in your path so that you can master the tough shots that you will certainly face on the golf course. For example, pick a spot on the range and imagine that you are replaying a shot that you mishit during a recent round of golf and try getting your shot to come as close to the spot as possible. Memorize the mechanics and feeling that you experience when you achieve your goal for that shot.

Place a ball next to a tree trunk and challenge yourself to hit the ball onto a particular spot on the fairway. Use different clubs to hit balls out of fairway bunkers to build memories that you can recall during an actual round. Don't just hit balls. Have a purpose to every practice regimen that you perform and stay with that practice regime until you experience both the mechanics and feeling of each shot.

Another part of developing discipline concerns your physical workout routine. Your legs need to be in good shape to maneuver the course. Your wrists need to be strong as do your forearms and biceps.

Power walking is effective as is weight training. Swinging golf clubs also depends on upper and lower body coordination and rhythm, which can be practiced regularly wherever you are. It is possible to improve your coordination and rhythm without even having a club in your hands. Throughout your physical workout routine and practice regimen you should strive to also develop the mental side of your game. This requires that you consciously strive to develop the right side of your brain. This is achieved by memorizing mental pictures and feelings.

Developing discipline concerning both mechanics and the mental activities can be aided by some easily achieved approaches. Some of them are:

• When performing your morning workout routine, change the order of your exercises every day.
• If your workout routine involves power walking or running use different routes every day.
• Consciously change the order of buttoning your clothing to create a different dressing routine.
• Periodically use different grips when practice putting to gain confidence in the grip that you use on the course for distance and accuracy.
• When you establish your daily, weekly and monthly schedules, consider your must do priorities for yourself as well as for work, family and others.
• Practice different length backswings to form mental pictures and feelings for each swing.
• Embrace stress that you experience, strive to

understand its cause and strive to develop mental pictures and feelings of effectively dealing with all types of stress.

My friend Roy, who wrote the Forward of this book, keeps detailed notes on his mechanical progress as well as his feelings. He does this to develop both sides of his brain. He writes as follows:

"I added a section to my 'Golf Lessons' file to give me a place to modify important points whenever I want to. Here are some examples: 'After keeping my personal golf lesson file current for about two years, I decided to read my file the evening before I play golf instead of during my round. Reading my file while I played golf was beginning to distract me.

While riding my stationary bike each morning, I read a golf magazine. After exercising, I go to my computer to capture my thoughts, which I enjoy doing.

I played in a tournament recently and scored a 90 with 45 putts. Later I thought that if I used only 32 putts, I would have scored a 77 and won the tournament.'"

This quote clearly demonstrates the need to become very much aware of your play as well as developing a sense of what to do to progress your game. You may not choose to take on this approach but I highly recommend that you develop one that suites you.

Practice set routines to develop a systematic practice schedule which can lead to developing a strategy for play

Just as it is important to have a strategy for playing a course, it is equally important to have a strategy for your practice sessions. Simply trying to hit shots with each of the clubs in your bag will usually not improve your game.

You should strive to be able to envision each good shot

that you have previously hit with every club during actual play on a golf course. When you are playing golf memorize the mechanics and feeling of each good shot as you watch your ball fly towards your target. Establish priorities both on the golf course as well as in your life and practice them consistently. Remember that putting your priorities in order in one area of your life will carryover into other areas.

Each club can be used to hit very different shots. Developing the right side of your brain by memorizing mechanics as well as feelings during practice sessions can help you improve your golf game tremendously. During actual play, your right brain portfolio of shots will over time automatically enable you to envision the exact shot that you must hit for any given situation. Prior to each round you should strive to develop a strategic plan for playing the course. This is a left brain activity that should be written down. The right brain activity that surfaces the best tactics for each shot will automatically come to you during your round if you have developed the mental side of your game.

Clearing your mind of distracting issues, thoughts and feelings that might interfere with maintaining your focus and staying in your zone

The carryover effect from one experience to another experience has a great deal to do with your performance. The carryover effect concerns the transfer of knowledge gained during one of your life's experiences to another life experience. Developing the right side of your brain for the game of golf will enable you to be more creative. Solving a golf puzzle on the course will enable you to improve your puzzle solving ability for other areas of your life.

Carrying a bad day at work home with you that results

in taking out your frustrations on your family is an example of a negative carryover effect that you can learn to avoid. Carrying positive feelings and mental pictures that you experience at work home with you can produce a positive calming effect on your family. Also, learn to envision what you want your family relationship to be upon your arrival. The key is to learn how to develop the right side of your brain to always memorize positive visions and feelings. You can learn to consider negative experiences as challenges to overcome. In this manner, negative experiences become positive experiences.

The carryover effect holds true for the game of golf as well as all other sports. Developing the right side of your brain to produce positive golf visions and the left side of your brain to creatively solve golf puzzles will carryover to other life situations. The more you are able to carryover positive visions and feelings from other parts of your life into your golf game the more successful you will be. By the same token, if you carryover negative visions and feelings into your golf game, the less successfully you will play.

Some people don't know how clear their minds of negative thoughts thoughts. Before each practice session try this mind clearing technique. Close your eyes and imagine being back in school. Imagine a blackboard that is used by several teachers, none of whom bothered to erase it. It is extremely cluttered and confusing. Slowly begin to erase the blackboard. The key to this exercise is performing it slowly. When you have erased the blackboard, envision that you then use wet cloth to clear any chalk dust that might still be on the blackboard.

Wait for the blackboard to dry and look at the clean surface. Your mind has been cleared. Now you can proceed with your golf game in a relaxed, focused, enjoyable and productive manner. Learning how to clear your mind will produce great benefits.

Developing a Relaxed and Confident Attitude That Will Carryover Into Competitive Golf

Your practice regimen is not an end unto itself. Its purpose is to help you develop sound golf swing fundamentals along with the right side of your brain. An important part of each practice session is to practice relaxation and confidence building techniques. The more you effectively use your practice regimen to improve your swing fundamentals as well as your visioning ability, the more relaxed you will become. If you are tense or anxious about a shot, you won't be able to hit it as well as when you are completely relaxed. This is because you will probably doubt your ability to hit the shot. It certainly means that you have not developed the right side of your brain. If your hand trembles a bit while you are standing over a putt, this indicates that you are transferring your anxiety to your body.

The more you practice swing fundamentals and visioning techniques, the more relaxed you will become. The more relaxed you become, the more confident you will feel.

It's that simple. Achieving these feelings should become part of every practice session. Prior to one of his tournaments, Arnold Palmer closed his car door on one of his fingers, which he had to bandage. Although it was painful, he said that it helped him relax his grip and he subsequently won the tournament.

Developing a feel for accomplishments in practice to help you stay in your zone

I can't emphasize this point enough. Referring back to my comments on the left and right sides of the brain, remember how your conscious efforts can, with consistent practice over time, become part of an effortless routine that you can call upon when needed. When you look into the eyes of a professional golfer, you can get a sense of whether he/she is in his/her zone or is struggling. The ability to staying in your zone is developed during your practice regimen.

You really shouldn't experiment while playing a round. Playing the game is where you should be using what you have learned and have come to feel during your practice regimen.

When you are able to envision good shots while playing a round of golf, you have a tool that can help you execute shot-after-shot with precision and confidence.

You have probably experienced this from time-to-time. Developing the mental side of golf will enable you to consistently experience new positive feelings when you play every round of golf.

It takes a great deal of self-discipline to maintain focus and stay in your zone.

Staying in your zone is that sense of having a feel for your performance, while remaining focused on performing the mechanics of each golf swing.

It also includes being able to manage outside influences, such as stress in your personal life as well as any stress you may encounter while playing the game. A good friend of mine refers to me as the "Zone Coach" because of the amount of importance I place on staying in your zone.

Recognize
Your Assets
and Liabilities

If you were to approach a gym for the first time, you might be evaluated by a professional trainer to determine what type of physical routine will work best for you. The professional trainer recognizes that one person may require a certain type of workout while someone else might benefit from another. It is usually recommended that people start out slowly and gradually work up to increasing their weights and repetitions while exercising. Developing a healthy body takes place over time and everyone approaches it differently. Everyone has their strong and weak points that need to be assessed and taken into consideration for them to attain their desired goal. Attempting to go beyond these limits could result in permanent physical injury and defeat their whole purpose. You might even conclude you have failed instead of realizing that you were just in over your head.

Your expectations and priorities must to be clear, realistic and attainable. Otherwise, you are operating on an uneven playing field, which will probably result in competing against yourself, which always slows down your progress. You must practice patience and persistence. There is no instant approach to anything worthwhile.

Confidence is defined as believing in yourself and believing that what you believe is true.

When you believe in something that is not true or attainable, you might think you are confident but you are really setting yourself up for failure. What you consider to be true and what you can actually do must be one-and-the-same. You can believe and expect that you can do something but if it is not realistic and within the range of your ability, problems are sure to result.

In the game of golf, the very same principle applies. You must learn to recognize your ability scale (potential). No two people have the same ability scale. It takes time and practice to improve your game of golf and advance in the sport. Premature or undue expectations might result in becoming impatient with your progress and cause you to reach unreasonable conclusions about your game.

Some people become so frustrated with their play that they quit or might bend a few clubs around the nearest tree. There is nothing wrong with realizing that you aren't doing well in certain parts of the game. It may take an evaluation by a golf professional to understand how to correct or improve problems. Your progress needs to be measured in steps and gauged over a reasonable period of time before it will become lasting progress. Sinking a difficult putt once and celebrating your achievement doesn't mean that you will be able to repeat that putt consistently. This will take time, patience and practice. Golf professionals will tell you that:

"The more you practice, the luckier you will get."

If the game of golf teaches anything, it teaches humility, patience and persistence, all of which have to do with how effectively you use your mind. *Be kind to yourself.*

Remember, that if you're not having any fun playing the game, something is probably wrong with your attitude and expectations. It is not the result of having the wrong clubs, your score or your potential. Probably, your best bet would be to get to a competent instructor, who can evaluate your problem objectively instead of taking on a negative, self punishing attitude. You are worth it. Realizing that your personal view of a problem with your game might deserve a more objective evaluation takes a good deal of maturity and self-confidence. There's nothing wrong with admitting that you are human and need some help.

Perfection
vs. Excellence

Another meaning of the term mental is to indicate that someone is crazy. I have heard it said that people who play golf must be crazy to chase a little white ball around and suffer the frustration that the game of golf brings. By the same token, the saying *"A bad day on the course is better than a good day in the office."* suggests that satisfaction can be gained from playing the game while enjoying the out-of-doors. Another saying is that *"Just one good shot keeps us coming back to playing the game once again."* I know that is true in my case but by the same token, I want to develop a consistency in my game and not just be satisfied with an occasional celebration.

One thing very clear is that golf is not a game in which perfection can be achieved. A colleague of mine, Dr. Bob Rotella, has an excellent series on various aspects of golf. In one of his presentations, he coined the phrase, *"Golf is not a game of perfect."* I find it interesting that golf tends to attract people that possess perfectionist traits. This seems reasonable, since the game of golf requires a great deal of precision to play the game well. I am always amused during the broadcast of a tournament when an announcer proclaims, *"That was a perfect shot."* When applied to players like Tiger Woods or Phil Mickelson, it is particularly interesting because people tend to view their games as perfect. People become upset when Tiger and Phil don't make the shots they are supposed to make. Tiger Woods commented about a putt that wormed its way into the hole on a very uneven green that it was all luck. Tiger's comment defused the announcer's statement of perfection.

At the 2006 U.S. Open, a great deal of media attention was paid to the fact that Tiger Woods missed the cut for the first time in his professional career. The media felt that the month's layoff from competition that Tiger took after his father's death was the cause. There was also a great deal of attention paid to the fact that Phil Mickelson blew his lead because of a poor judgment call and lost the tournament. Why is it that some people are so quick to pick up on the negatives? Tiger and Phil are human. They are not perfect.

Consider, too, the comeback of Paul Azinger, another excellent golfer. After doing battle with cancer he managed to score well in tournaments after his recovery. His abilities and knowledge of the game have earned him the privilege of being the next Captain of the 2008 Ryder Cup. Not one of us is safe from the stressors that life brings and in that sense we all share in our humanity. It is how well we deal with adversity that can make the difference. Other people may judge us harshly and unfairly while using standards of perfection but only we know what we have undergone and the toll that we've had to pay.

Perfection is unachievable. Perfection is a fantasy that some people believe is attainable for one reason.

The need for perfection doesn't come from being human; it comes from unwillingness to accept our humanity.

This is why some people beat themselves up or criticize others whenever a mistake is made. I have seen a golfer go into a rage when he made a mistake calling himself stupid over and over again.

Not only can perfection not be achieved, but also those who seek perfection are never satisfied with any of their accomplishments because nothing is ever good enough. Some people believe that is how to improve and win or seeking perfection is the key to competing more success-fully. Think about it. How can anyone accomplish any results by using negative thinking as a base? You just can't achieve anything positive from something that is negative. It is unrealistic to expect positive results to come from negativity. It is a "Catch 22" from which it is very difficult to escape from both on the golf course as well as life in general.

There is this story: "I dreamt I died and went to Heaven and was sitting talking with God. God sneezed and I didn't know what to say." Even if you consider golf a sport, it is still a game. I emphasize the word game because golf does not allow anyone to achieve a perfect score. Think about it. It is possible to get a perfect 300 score in bowling but there is no such thing as a perfect score in golf. A friend joked that in order to have a perfect score, you must shoot a hole-in-one on each hole for a total score of 18. A score of 18 is highly improbable, if not impossible.

Sharpening your skills allows for endless oppor-tunities to progress.

There is no such thing as mastering the game of golf because everyone makes mistakes. There is always some-thing new to learn about the game of golf. This is what draws you back to playing the game. In tournament play, the player who makes the fewest mistakes usually wins the tournament. However, think of what you go through when you have problems dealing with your own mistakes. Do you take them in stride or become self-critical for not being perfect?

Then the golf game becomes both agonizing and self-limiting. It is very difficult to focus on your game when you're so deeply affected by making a mistake. Save yourself the aggravation and come out of the land of perfection. Enter the land of humanity. Chuck Yeager, the famous pilot, used the term *"Press On!"* which could well be applied to the game of golf.

Something else that is interesting about perfection is that you can't win for losing. If you are a perfectionist, you have probably noticed that the more you try to be perfect, the more mistakes you make. Striving for perfection is very stressful and produces tension that interferes with whatever you're doing. I think the Germans have a saying that goes something like, *"The harder you try, the behinder you get."* Many of us carry tendencies from childhood into our adult lives. Can you see how this problem would hinder your progress? In my work with golfers the problem is very real and more common than most people realize.

So, where does this bring us? We have noted that golfers with varying degrees of perfectionist tendencies play a game that doesn't have a perfect score. Probably the best thing they can do is to give it up. No, I don't mean that you should give up the game but maybe you should be more realistic about your personal goals for the game of golf. To achieve excellence is a realistic goal. Most people don't realize the difference between excellence and perfection.

Perfection doesn't allow people to rebound after making a mistake because the concepts of mistake and perfection can not co-exist. A perfectionist doesn't believe that he/she has any choices. However, excellence does allow people to make and correct their mistakes or rebound from them because there is room for other choices. While perfection is not attainable, excellence results from doing your best on any given day. I have found that a sense of humor helps people place their perfectionist tendencies into a more reasonable perspective. Being able to laugh at ourselves is probably the best therapy that we can experience.

Dealing With Mindsets and Slumps

Before I begin describing my experience in working with a slumping golfer, I first want to define a slump.

A slump is simply a state of mind resulting in believing that you can't achieve something that you have already accomplished.

It is a psychological state of doubt that has nothing to do with your abilities or technical grasp of the game. It is a series of repetitive mind sets. Some golfers believe that they can get out of a slump by practicing more or simply changing their routine.

Although these approaches may be important remedies, few people know that it is really how they use their mind and how they focus on aspects of their performance that cures a slump. The key to dealing with a slump is to relax, recall when you previously accomplished the task successfully and then envision that accomplishment. Do this as many times as you feel are necessary before you actually perform the task again. This is another example of the power of the mental side of the game of golf. Mind relaxation exercises are described in the *"Relaxation, Visualization and Imagery Training"* chapter of the book.

There was a golf pro and manager of a private club who wanted to improve his putting. He wanted to qualify for the PGA Tour. He was having problems sinking 10 foot putts. I met with him a couple of times and observed that he demanded a great deal of himself. When he didn't perform according to his expectations, he would get down on himself. He was a perfectionist.

I agreed to observe him play nine holes on his home course. When the ball came within ten feet of the hole, he would freeze up and miss the putt. He would line the ball up well but would break down when executing the shot. This prevented a smooth putting stroke. He had the yips; however, even with his poor putting problem, he remarkably shot below par.

I only made a few comments throughout his play because I was focusing on assessing his mental approach to putting. On the tees and fairways he went through a repetitious mind ritual that enabled him to strike the ball towards his target very accurately. He made some audible mutterings and had a slight waggle prior to striking the ball, which seemed to give him a sense of confidence.

It isn't unusual for many golfers to go through repetitive motions before striking a ball, which can become a helpful tool. Some players take one or more practice swings while others stand behind the ball to determine distance, direction, club selection and trajectory. Still others plant their feet a one or more times before putting and some perform a little waggle prior to striking the ball. There is nothing wrong with these rituals if they serve the purpose of building readiness and confidence.

However, when it came time for the golfer to putt the ball, instead of creating a positive mental attitude, his ritual seemed to reinforce his doubt and negativity. I could see his frustration build as he doubted himself. His putting ritual was different than the ones he used on the tee or fairway. He believed that his different putting ritual would rid him of his yips. But instead of relaxing him he became even tenser as he anticipated missing another putt. He was creating a repetitive pattern of failure.

After a well-placed iron shot to the 6th green, his ball landed about 10 feet from the hole. He was about to address the ball for his birdie attempt when I stopped him just after he completed his ritual. Although my interruption seemed to bother him, he looked at me and waited for my next comment.

I said: "For this putt, I want you to reverse the position of your right and left hands on your putter; then I want you to stand to the side of your ball and take two practice swings while you envision your ball traveling along the line that you have chosen and going into the hole." He did what I asked and his putt went on his putting line to dead center of the hole.

Apart from my instruction, I asked him what the difference was in his sinking the putt that way instead of the usual way. He replied "There is really no difference, both approaches will work." We talked about the fact that I interrupted him during his putting setup, which wasn't working for him. I recommended that he find his own way of interrupting his putting setup until he found a positive pattern that produced the results he wanted. Notice that I didn't recommend my approach but suggested that he develop his own. Not only did his perfection goal not allow him to rebound, his goal reinforced his pattern of failure. How frustrating that must have been for him. A few weeks later, he phoned me and reported that his putting problem was fixed.

I asked him to change his mechanical approach to putting to cause him to use the right side of his brain to recall his visions of prior successes. Later he practiced different putting mechanics but he finally succeeded when he remembered how to cycle back and forth between the left and right sides of his brain.

Mind sets that are entrenched in the left side of the brain tend to make people stubborn. Even though they actually interfere with your performance, you will only be able to change them if you switch to the right side of your brain to surface new visions. This approach will shortly enable you to feel comfortable with change.

Change is difficult. The more you learn to cause and accept productive change as part of life, the more you will be able to achieve your goals. If you believe that you won't be able to constructively improve what you are doing, you have probably never learned how to or have forgotten how to use the right side of your brain.

Recall the exercises that will help you clear the left side of your brain to allow you to use the right side of your brain to cause and finally accept constructive change. Always look inside yourself before drawing conclusions about unwanted patterns in your golf game or life in general. You have the ability to surface your answers. You need to learn how to relax and allow answers to come out of the right side of your brain instead of just pushing engrained mind sets. Everyone can develop this power. Learn to work with and trust both sides of your brain.

A Manly Golfer's Grip

A competitive golfer came to me after spending considerable time taking lessons to cure a problem she was having with her putter. The problem was assessed by her golf instructor as being caused by her grip. She bought new grips and changed her putting mechanics many times. When I greeted her with a handshake, I felt that her grip was as firm as a man's grip. I complemented her strong grip and she thanked me. Then, I said that she should consider using a gentler grip. I wanted to get her attention because she strongly believed that she still needed more lessons and equipment. When I continued to talk with her, I sensed that she enjoyed risk taking and was a bit of a daredevil but at the same time she needed to be in control.

Once I gained her attention, I asked her to please give me a putting lesson on her home course. She thought this to be a strange request but complied because she was curious about what I wanted to do. She certainly wasn't going to let me gain the upper hand. During my lesson, she worked with my stance, head position, reading the green and, finally, my grip. I intentionally gripped the putter with a death grip. I said that this tight grip had always helped me feel like I was going to succeed.

She asked me to loosen my grip but I loosened only a little bit each time and missed most of my putts. She chastised me and said that I apparently was not receptive to a necessary change. Clearly, she was very frustrated with me. I said that I was frustrated as well and asked that she show me how to do it. I set up five golf balls at different locations and distances from the cup and told her that I would watch while she stroked each of them into the cup.

She began by gripping her club tightly as she usually did, but knowing that I was watching intently, she consciously relaxed her grip. By the time she struck the fifth ball her grip and stroke were more relaxed. She missed several of her first putts but sank her putts as her grip became naturally relaxed. She gave me a big grin when she finished and begrudgingly said, "OK, I get the message." We did some more work in my office around the use of relaxation techniques prior to her putting to clear the left side of her brain. We also worked on visioning techniques with the right side of her brain to cause her to recall her prior positive visions.

Later, she wrote me a note of thanks indicating that she will always remember me and that the techniques I taught her were working consistently for all of her shots. I thoroughly enjoyed working with this very interesting woman.

The Art of Reframing and Rebounding

Many times, when you form a mechanics mind set while in the course of play or even while you are practicing at the range, you might find it very difficult to break out of your mind set. When you have tried to relax and replace your negative thinking with a positive vision, your slump may still persist. This might mean that you may not have practiced clearing the left side of your brain enough times to allow positive visions from the right side of your brain to surface. Without new positive visions it is difficult to use the left side of your brain to work on swing fundamentals (mechanics) that will ultimately enable you to get out of your slump. This can become more and more frustrating and will tend to reinforce itself to the point that the harder you try to get out of your slump, the more you might entrench your slump.

Continuing to push the envelope by telling yourself that you should try harder or employ what your golf instructor might have taught you to do to correct your golf swing mechanics might actually reinforce your slump instead of finding a way for you to get out of it. There are usually many causes for this. You might be trying too hard to practice your golf swing fundamentals. Or you might unconsciously be trying to kill the ball to get more distance. Or you may simply be putting too much pressure on yourself. What is really important is finding a way out of the problematic pattern that has taken over your game of golf. The solution usually involves the mental side of golf.

Occasionally, when you are playing a casual round of golf on your home course and you are not satisfied with your game, try not playing a difficult hole. Instead, clear the left side of your brain with a relaxation technique and then walk or ride the hole and *play it mentally* by recalling visions of your most probable shots. For example, if you typically slice the ball off the tee and land about 175 yards ahead in the right rough, envision that you have taken your stance on the right side of the tee, aimed 175 yards ahead to the left side of the fairway. Then envision that you hit your typical slice off the tee and that, because of your stance, your ball lands 175 yards ahead on the right center of the fairway.

Imagine that the hole that you selected to play mentally is a 500 yard par 5 hole. Therefore, you are 325 yards away from the green. Let's also assume that you really know that you rarely hit your fairway woods well but you are pretty good with your middle irons. Imagine that you have selected a 4 iron for your second shot. Envision that you have taken a stance to the left of your ball and take two half-practice swings concentrating on the feeling you experience when you hit down and through the ball. Then mentally take your stance and envision that you hit your ball 165 yards straight down the center of the fairway. Now you are 160 yards from the green.

Let's assume that whenever you are faced with a mid iron shot to the green you miss the green 75% of the time. However, you are usually very accurate with your short irons, which is generally the saving grace of your game. Imagine that you have selected a 7 iron for your third shot.

You typically hit your 7 iron 140 yards but occasionally you hit it 160 yards when you are in your zone. Again, envision that you have taken a stance to the left of your ball and take two half-practice swings concentrating on the feeling you experience when you hit down and through the ball. Then mentally take your stance and envision that you hit your ball 150 yards straight down the center of the fairway to the apron of the green. Now you are 10 yards from the green.

Select the iron that you typically chip with from the lie and distance from the hole that you have envisioned. Again, envision that you have taken a stance to the left of your ball and take two half practice chips concentrating on the feeling you experience when you take a short backswing, don't cock your wrists and hit smoothly down, accelerate through the ball and stop your chip when the head of your club is about thigh high. Envision that you ball stops 6 feet from the hole.

Mentally look at your imaginary ball from the front, back and both sides. Mentally imagine that you walk with your putter to your ball and take two 100% practice putts from the side of your ball. Step up to your ball and putt it along the line that you have chosen. Imagine that you putt rims out of the cup leaving you a tap in for a bogey 6. As you walk away from the green, you make the commitment to work on your putting stroke to ensure that you make your par from that distance 75% of the time in the future.

Now go to the next hole with your foursome and begin playing golf again. Repeat everything that you did on the prior imaginary hole. Only this time actually hit the ball.

The practice hole that you just played mentally should awaken your skill to use both sides of your brain. On the next hole you will more likely be able to stay within your capabilities as you use both sides of your brain along with your swing mechanics to play and enjoy the game of golf.

Mentally playing holes on your course should not be a sign of giving up on yourself or your game. It is a means of reframing your mind to use both sides of your mind. Being able to work on a problem mentally can often provide the answer to that problem.

Your slump is not the problem. Slumps occur when people focus on negatives instead of positives. A positive approach is the only way that most problems can be resolved.

Instead of consciously trying to find the cure, walking away helps us call on what we already know to surface alternative solutions. Don't forget that you weren't always in a slump. In effect, mentally playing a hole enabled you to move toward a positive solution instead of continuing your negative mode. Remember that you must use both sides of your brain and be able to cycle back and forth. And remember too, that a slump is a function of how your mind might be working against you. Learning to clear your left brain so that you can surface right brain visions will help you make progress not only in the game of golf but also for solving life's problems as well.

The entire educational system stresses left brain activities. The game of golf is an excellent venue to help you develop the right side of your brain as well. Accomplishing this goal will certainly increase your enjoyment of the game of golf, while also helping you enjoy solving life's challenges.

Here's a method that I'd like for you to try when you forget whatever it is that you need to know. Every time you have a problem remembering something, you probably try very hard to consciously think of what it is. Instead of doing this, I suggest that you clear the left side of your brain with your favorite relaxation technique and move onto something else in your mind or some other form of activity. When you do this, and when you least expect it, you will remember whatever it is that you needed to know. This method rarely fails.

Just be patient and trust that one or the other sides of your brain will remember what you needed to know.

Being able to clear the left side of your brain so that you can utilize both sides of your brain will get you out of more jams than you can imagine. You can use both sides of your brain to get out of a slump in the game of golf or to solve life's challenges as well. Using both sides of your brain improves rational thought, which is a left brain activity and all types of creative thinking, which is a right brain activity. These powers can be part of everyone's mind. It is simply a matter of developing them.

Your Expectations of Yourself

Probably one of the most troublesome parts of life has to do with your expectations of yourself.

Unreasonable expectations tend to promote a sense of failure while diminishing your success.

This applies to every area of life. In golf, unreasonable expectations might lead to: undue pressure, tension, anxiety, frustration, anger, fear, doubt, negative thinking, mental and sometimes physical imbalance, poor performance and an attitude problem, just to name a few.

Try putting those problems into your bag and carry them around for 18 holes. Imagine what your success rate will be. How can you play a game that calls for precision while facing all those problems? The answer is you can't. Forget about it. You will be defeated before you take your first swing. And the exact same thing happens in life as well. Instead, you learn to envision reasonable expectations and practice to achieve them consistently. Remember too, that if you are accustomed to living your life with unreasonable expectations, you will carry that practice into your golf game as well.

For a beginning golfer to break 100, he/she must score a bogey on nine holes and a double bogey on the remaining nine holes. If a golfer has never broken 100, why should he/she worry about scoring par on any hole? This is not to say that you shouldn't want to improve. The real issue is whether you are demanding something of yourself that can't be achieved within the framework of your present abilities and level of competence.

Continuing to play the game of golf and improve your swing fundamentals along with the mental side of the game so that you will be able to move to a higher level. This is a reasonable and achievable expectation and something that can be attained over time with an effective practice regimen. Seek the advice of a golf instructor you trust and consider working with a coach, who can help you with the mental side of your game.

Visualizing a task in slow motion is also a helpful tool. Fear can be dealt with in the same manner. Everyone has fears. Perhaps you have a fear of executing certain shots. First, see yourself facing that fear in your mind by performing the shot until you succeed. You will eventually perform it on the course as well.

Practicing swing fundamentals along with mental exercises to develop both sides of your brain to correct whatever the problem is that is causing your fear will help. Please consider the following saying:

"Excitement is only fear that we choose to challenge."

Although this is a truism, when you consider what happens when you become excited about something, you are probably taking a risk to overcome one or more of life's fears. This is a very interesting way to view and practice overcoming fears. The feedback I have received from people indicates that this approach works. Sometimes, you can move into a mind set that prevents you from executing shots without even being aware that you have a problem. That mind set probably is probably caused by some type of fear.

Some people adopt the attitude of not trying something new to avoid failure and not even realize that they are experiencing fear. If you don't recognize you have a problem and clearly identify it, you won't be able to correct it. Always be aware of your feelings and label them correctly. Interestingly, others may resist dealing with their fears because, if they are successful, they might be expected to perform similarly on a consistent basis. Perfectionists typically don't take many chances because they fear failure.

Also, please keep in mind that your feelings are neither positive nor negative and neither good nor bad. They are just feelings. Feelings can't hurt you or anyone else for that matter. Feelings are indicators that something is going on that needs attention. Some people mistakenly believe that their feelings are the problem that they are experiencing.

It is really not your feelings but rather the methods by which you handle them that grow into problems. If you have a fear of hitting over water, rather than making believe that the fear doesn't exist, it is better identify it and face it so that you can overcome your fear. I speak from personal experience. For years I was afraid of water holes but now water holes don't faze me. They are just part of the game of golf and a challenge that once faced has allowed me to be successful (for the most part) in dealing with that hazard. My fear has now become a challenge.

Knowing what you are feeling and being able to label it correctly is important for all feelings. Let's take the feeling of uncertainty in choosing which club to use in a particular situation. That is not uncommon. You have probably been uncertain about your club selection one time or another. Try recalling that situation and the feeling you had when you successfully made your choice. **BINGO**! Now you have a reference point that can help you. However, if you are oblivious to your feelings, every situation will appear to be new, different and strange and you will need to re-invent each shot without having the benefit of that reference point. The game of golf is difficult and challenging enough without making it more difficult.

Learning How to Develop a Feel for the Game

On one occasion, my wife and I were placed with another golfing couple whom we had never met. The husband was an excellent golfer who parred just about every hole and birdied two or three of them. It was evident that they were accomplished golfers and I was particularly impressed with his wife, who was quite petite. Prior to striking the ball, she had no practice swing or hesitation of any kind. She merely addressed the ball and swung the club in an easy, fluid motion, which resulted in advancing her ball to a very playable position.

Her pace was impressive and the competition she had going with her husband was amusing. Her drives were straight and consistently flew 170 to 185 yards onto the fairway. Clearly, she was having fun and her attitude was positive and forgiving whenever she made a mistake. Instead of allowing her mistakes to disarm her solid play, she would easily rebound from them. Her sense of humor and the good natured competitive banter that went on between the couple didn't interfere with her focus either.

In addition to being very focused and in her zone, she had put her game together and performed without any observable conscious effort. She was not preoccupied with the mechanics of how she should execute each shot. Her approach to the game was that of being relaxed and having fun. I sensed that she tended to recall the positive results of past play and brought it into the present. In effect, she had developed a feel for the game. Her game was not the same as her husband's, mine or my wife's game. She was aware of and trusted her feelings because they worked for her in the past and presently as well. We later chatted about my observations which she said were accurate.

Once again, I'd like to quote my friend Roy's excerpt from his golf diary. Roy is expert at the mental side of golf and takes the time to write down his feelings along with swing fundamentals that he thinks are important. There are many methods that people use to develop both sides of their brain to play and enjoy the game of golf according to their abilities. An excerpt from Roy's diary follows:

"Your stance and body should be parallel to your putting line. Both wrists should be slightly bent which is the proper position for any golf grip. Your weight should be on the center of your right foot and you should feel like you are tossing your right palm towards the hole during your putting movement. Your arms should swing like a pendulum. Swing the club slowly back until it reaches your right foot, then swing the club forward with a slightly accelerating swing, making sure that the club face is perpendicular to the ball for at least as long as it takes the club face to reach your left foot.

Note that Roy describes one of the feelings that he has experienced while he is putting. Again, your approach to progressing in your putting routine may be quite different but it may work well for you. If you decide to change your approach, you will need to spend some time with that change before it becomes more natural. Then, you may decide to change it once again at another time. You might even decide to go back to your initial approach if you find that the new approaches don't feel quite right. It's all up to you and what feels right and works best for you. There's no one size fits all formula that can be applied.

Two additional experiences demonstrate that golf is clearly based on the feel that you develop for the game and that thinking only about your score and the mechanics of swing fundamentals might actually restrict your progress. Some golf professionals recommend that golfers forget about each shot and just hit it. Their theory is that your body will automatically recall what it has been programmed to do during your practice sessions.

One experience dates back to when I was in my late 20's. At that age I took golf lessons from an instructor because I had only dabbled in the game of golf prior to that time and felt more frustration than satisfaction when I was on the course. I went to a manager of a small driving range, who also gave golf lessons. A condition of his teaching was that you were only allowed to use your 5 iron during practice sessions based on his theory that if you could master your 5 iron, you would be able to do the same thing with every other club in your bag. I signed up for five 30 minute lessons.

By the fourth lesson He had taught me to regularly and consistently hit my 5 iron 165 yards straight out to my target. He worked with my stance, grip, and swing fundamentals. However, whenever I struck the ball well, he would always ask me how I felt at the top of my backswing. He contended that the top of your backswing demonstrates that everything else about the process of striking the ball is in order. He wanted me to memorize that feeling. In the fifth and last session, he directed me to address the ball but not swing the club. After doing so, I waited for his next directive. He said nothing. Instead, he blindfolded me and said: "Now take your swing and hit the ball".

I objected but he interrupted me saying that my practice with my 5 iron wasn't only to teach the technical aspects of hitting a consistently accurate ball. He went on to say: "I have taught you how to get a feel for your swing and impact. If you recall your correct feeling at the top of your backswing, you will hit it. If you don't recall that feeling, you won't hit a good shot." Then, once again, he directed me to swing the club. Just after the point of impact, he whipped the blindfold off and, sure enough, the ball traveled 165 yards straight at my target.

I will never forget that experience and now I am passing that same sense of performing a shot to you. The mechanical aspects of your game will help you gain consistency but your feel for the shot will ensure your progress. The basis for gaining that feel was not only the repetitions of swinging the 5 iron the same way each time but also memorizing the feeling I experienced when I hit a shot properly. The instructor taught me how to use the right side of my brain. I can still recall that feeling even though I took those lessons more than thirty years ago. You can experience that same feeling by lining up a practice putt and closing your eyes before striking the ball. You might be surprised with your outcome.

The next experience is a very recent one. I have a good friend who comes to Florida a couple of times every year and we make it a point to play as much golf as we can while he is here. He lives in a four season climate that usually has severe winters so he comes to Florida to play golf. We were behind a very slow foursome, who dramatically slowed down our pace and tempo and we shot rather poorly for the first several holes. We began play during the mid-afternoon so that by the time we reached the 10th hole, darkness was almost upon us. And so we decided to re-play the first five holes since no one else was playing them. We decided to just have some fun while working our way back to the clubhouse. To shorten the story, we both shaved 8-10 strokes off our original scores.

No matter what the sport, I always tell clients that

"The greatest learning we can achieve is when we don't know we are learning and when we are having fun."

It is obvious to me that there is a difference between someone playing a sport who truly loves what he/she is doing versus someone who is doing it just for the sake of doing it or for financial gain. Enjoying your play and having fun can make the difference between a good or poor performance and that is a very important point to remember.

What You See Is What You Get

"What you see is what you get." is an old saying that means we shouldn't expect anything more than what our vision and perception sees as reality. I am using this saying to show that you not only see with your eyes but also see with your mind as well. You are probably aware that both your eyes and mind can play tricks on you. As an example, you have probably experienced driving down the road believing that you are seeing water ahead on the road only to find that it was a mirage created by the reflection angle of the sun. Or you might have experienced choosing the wrong club because the pin appears much farther or closer than it really is. Or your fear of hitting over water might indeed result in your ball taking an unnecessary bath. Many of us have been there, haven't we?

Dealing with a difficult shot may not just be based on what you are about to encounter but mixed in might be some feelings that tend to complicate your perception as well as your attempt. Just as your feelings can fog perception, they can enhance your perception as well. When you feel positive and confident, your chances of successfully executing a difficult shot will be more assured.

When small children encounter new situations, they are not plagued by doubt or fear. Instead, their attitude is *"I can do that!"* The key word here is **DOING!** For adults, facing doubts and fears is not easily experienced. You need to have your mind go back to the time in your life when you experienced similar doubts and fears. Everyone has experienced doubts and fears. Possibly, someone in your life went overboard in wanting you to exercise caution and as a result they may have unwittingly put a damper on your sense of adventure and risk-taking.

Remember that excitement is only fear that we choose to challenge, The way you think, feel and act affects your performance in either positive or negative ways. Excitement is what children feel a great deal. Excitement can influence how you see things, your performance and the outcome. In other words, what your mind and eyes see may either be positive or it can result with your falling into the very trap that you want to avoid. It is not the feelings that you experience that become the problem. Rather, it is the manner in which you have learned to handle them that can either result in a good or poor shot.

Problems experienced in golf are often indicative of similar problems dealing with issues in your life. Learning how to deal with our problematic thoughts, feelings and view of life can mean the difference between success and failure both in terms of managing your life as well as in your golf game.

When I was practicing psychotherapy, I would ask clients to get up from their chair and stand in all four corners of the room to help them understand that looking at things from different points of view helps them understand their problem as well as the choices they have for resolving that problem. They would end up sitting in my chair, which helped them realize that they, not I, would accomplish their goal. My role was to help; theirs was to do.

This applies to golf as well. The more alternatives you can develop, the greater the chances of solving any problem. Why don't you try sitting in the four corners of your room and then right smack in the middle to get a sense of the lesson it provides?

If you duff a shot that finds its way into the woods resulting in having to take a drop and add a stroke, how you view and feel about that situation will clearly influence how you end up approaching and executing your next shot. If you experience a sense of defeat believing that you can't rebound from your mistake, then your mental vision of the next shot will be affected in a negative manner. However, if you can adopt the attitude that you have been there before, forget about the mistake and the extra stroke and focus on your positive strategy of hitting your next shot accurately, the result will be quite different. When your mental side takes on a positive perspective the result will be more positive. **PRESS ON**!

Also, consider the attitude that a bad shot isn't going to have one bit of influence on the outcome of your life. It is over and done with and nothing can be done to change it. But you can do something about the next shot and the outcome of your game. Learn how to let go and get on with it. The twelve step program cites *"Let go and let God."* Maybe your motto should be *"Let go and swing."*

I found Tiger Woods' idea of having some fun to be very interesting. As a youngster, he would place his ball in a seemingly impossible position by a tree stump and then attempt to shoot par for that hole. The more difficult and challenging he made the shot, the more fun he experienced. I suppose that this might be a good example of the saying *"If it doesn't kill you, it will make you stronger."* Yes, it is possible to deal with obstacles and have fun at the same time. Tiger would purposely make it difficult for himself. This kind of training helps strengthen your resolve and toughens you up to deal with adversities that you face in the game of golf as well as in life. It is also a way to practice self-discipline which is a vital part of golf and life as well.

PRESS ON!

Using your mind to recover or rebound takes patience, training and dedication to changing your methods of handling your thoughts, feelings and the way you view your game. There is nothing wrong with going back over what caused a poor shot but obsessing about it and forming a negative attitude won't solve a thing. Remember, the cure for negative, doubtful, obsessive thinking is **DOING, NOT THINKING**. You can do something to change the execution of your next shot but not the last one.

Thinking vs. Doing

I now want to talk about a very important point separating dedicated golfers from those who may not put the effort into progressing in their game. When you first come upon something that I call new learning, the process of turning that into knowledge requires a good deal of thinking and doing. However, new learning does not mean that you now have knowledge because true knowledge comes from experiencing something repeatedly.

Experiential knowledge is gained through repetition of your positive visions. Learning positive visioning techniques is essential in order to deal with the mental game of golf.

For instance, if we buy thicker grips, change our putting routine or shorten our backswing there is a great deal of thinking that initially needs to go into making that change a permanent part of our knowledge and future performance.

Once we've established a new pattern by consciously thinking while we're changing it, repeating it will eventually lead to replacing it with the desired outcome. That is what professionals mean when they say: *"Forget about the shot."* When we don't need to think about it anymore, there's no experimentation anymore. Instead, there's just doing, executing, or just plain action. It is at that point that you have attained the knowledge that can be consistently repeated because now it is engrained in both sides of your brain. This is when you will be able to recall and accomplish without requiring much conscious thought or trying. That same process holds true for changing life management patterns as well.

What I have just described is what you can also call a *"feel for the game."* This is an unconscious or right brained visioning process resulting from committing what you've learned to memory and then through the experience of practicing it, transferring that learning into experiential knowledge. You can read a book and learn a great deal but you won't have any knowledge of the subject until you practice what you have learned. That is why in school, the natural sciences have laboratories as part of the learning experience so that you can conduct experiments to prove or disprove the theories learned the classroom.

The example I gave earlier about my taking lessons using a 5 iron and gaining a feel for the stance, grip, left arm straight, backswing, ball contact, follow-through, etc. were all practiced over and over again providing me with a **KNOWLEDGE** and **FEEL** for the whole process. Once that was committed to memory through consistent practice that knowledge was able to be repeated without thinking! Then I could relax, trust my mind and just DO. So, if my relaxing helped me to repeat the pattern without thinking, it stands to reason that the more relaxed I am while learning, the greater the chances are of being able to reach that point of just doing. It is always very interesting to me that my recollection of that experience occurs every time I use a 5 iron. There are some people who just can't trust that and struggle dealing with life a great deal. Anyone, though, can learn how to do it.

Occasionally, you might see a professional golfer remain at the position from which they just hit a poor shot and take several practice swings. They might stop at the top of their backswing and look at their hands, club position, etc. to refresh their memory of proper swing fundamentals and feeling. They are focusing on both the mechanical aspects as well as the feel of their swing and committing it to memory for the next time they use that club. The top of their backswing is the determining factor as to whether they will strike the ball to their liking or not. Although this appears to be a physical process, it is ultimately a mental process as well. They might go through that same motion several times before they are satisfied that they have refreshed their memory.

This lesson was really brought home to me after hitting the blindfolded shot that I mentioned earlier. However, I want to add that after I completed my lessons and played a round of golf, I thought that I had lost my "touch. When I went back to the range, my feeling came back because I associated my comfort level with being on the range. Additionally, my anxiety while playing a round interfered with what I had learned on the range and it took a little while for me to regain my memory and feeling.

In effect, my learning hadn't become knowledge yet. Again, the trick was transferring the feeling I experienced on the range to the golf course. New circumstances bring different factors into play that require some re-thinking to get back in the groove. After a time, repeated practice of the shot enabled me to duplicate the same effect on the course as I had experienced on the practice range.

The ability to rebound is your ability to play golf at your very best and not get down on yourself when you make a mistake. It is not the mistake that becomes your problem.

It is how we use both sides of our brain to recover what we know. Oftentimes, your play is connected to the manner in which you are thinking and your mental attitude. In tournament play, it isn't the person you're pitted against that you want to beat; it is the course that you want to beat. Change your focus from beating your opponent to realizing that it is the course that holds the challenge. It is the course that has a number called par for each hole.

Think, Feel, Act (Do)

At this point, there is an interesting phenomenon that I would like to introduce you to. It has to do with three basic elements of our makeup that govern most of our activities; namely, *thinking, feeling and doing.*

If one of those elements is giving you trouble, and you choose to change it, the other two will follow suite and change as well without having to address them. Let's say that the way you're feeling is affecting what and how you are thinking as well as the outcome of your action. If you choose to change your feeling, your thinking and what you are doing will also change automatically. Remember only you can change the manner in which you feel, think or act.

Let's say that you are playing a round of golf and you notice that you have moved into a negative pattern of thinking. The first thing you must do is be aware of that fact. Once you are aware, focus on the manner in which you are thinking and choose to change it. Notice that I suggest that you choose which means that you have a choice and you don't need to allow your negative thinking to take over and rule the outcome of whatever you are attempting to accomplish.

If you are on the approach to a green and start to think about the last time you misjudged a chip, the chances are that you are going to repeat the problem. However, if you can catch yourself in time and focus on a time that you were successful when you chipped onto the green, your thinking can change as well as how you feel about the upcoming shot and the outcome of the shot. It's not magic but it sure seems like it. Practice this exercise repeatedly and you will find that you will improve your game.

Playing Games with the Game of Golf

There should be a purpose to every practice exercise that you invent and it is important for you to stay with the practice regimen you choose until you feel a sense of comfort and confidence with your performance and you can repeat it time-after-time. Here are some fun games that you can play to improve both your mental and mechanical capabilities:

- EXERCISE: Pick an imaginary spot on the driving range and try getting your shot to come as close to it as possible.
  PURPOSE: Gauging distance and accuracy of shots.

- EXERCISE: Place the ball next to a tree trunk or another obstacle in the rough and challenge yourself to "hit out" onto a particular spot on the fairway.
  PURPOSE: Becoming accustomed to dealing with problems experienced in the course of play and rebounding from them.

- EXERCISE: Use a club higher than a sand wedge to get out of a fairway trap some distance from the green so as to shoot for distance.
  PURPOSE: Becoming accustomed to using imag-

inative and different approaches to getting out of trouble on a course.

• EXERCISE: Place a ball in a divot or other hazardous position on the grass or sand and hit onto the green.
PURPOSE: Making the shot more difficult sharpens your skills.

• EXERCISE: Place a number of balls around the cup in a circle situated on an uneven or undulating green and putt them in from the various angles into the cup.
PURPOSE: Improving your reading of putts as well as compensating for different angles to the cup.

• EXERCISE: Purchase a device or use a heavy tumbler to practice you putting at home or office.
PURPOSE: Making good use of spare time to sharpen putting skills.

• EXERCISE: Chip into a coffee can or wide mouthed cup from various distances and angles while gradually changing the receptacle to a smaller opening approximating the size of a putting cup and vary the height of your shots.
PURPOSE: Increase chipping accuracy by getting a feel for success.

• EXERCISE: Line six to ten balls up on the apron of the green about one foot apart and chip each ball into the cup with as little conscious thought as possible.

PURPOSE: Practice getting a feel for chipping and reproducing that feel without much thought.

• EXERCISE: Experiment with different clubs in your bag from the apron or approach to the green.

PURPOSE: Getting a feel for the various ways the ball approaches the cup (e.g. back or forward spins, straight on, etc.) as well as for a sense of distance and accuracy with each club in order to attain a variety of choices for future use.

• EXERCISE: On a practice tee, pick a spot about ten feet ahead; then hit the ball with each club in your bag to that point; then increase the distance by another ten feet, etc.

PURPOSE: Experiencing a different sense of accuracy and feel in determining distances with each club even though you might not use that particular club to hit for that distance while playing (e.g. using the driver to chip onto the green).

• EXERCISE: Off the tee or the approach to a green, choose whichever clubs you wish until you hit the ball successfully, and then close your eyes after addressing the ball just before you strike it.

PURPOSE: Determine your feel for the rhythm, pace and distance in striking the ball with each club while paying attention to the top of your backswing.

• EXERCISE: Practice putting from as many different angles and distances from the cup as possible.

PURPOSE: Sharpening your skill of hitting the ball into the center of the cup.

• EXERCISE: Invent several practice games involving overcoming obstacles to successful completion.
PURPOSE: Getting used to the idea that the game of golf is always a challenge, which you take on with gusto; and then apply that lesson to your life.

• EXERCISE: Vary your takeaway speed and height of your backswing.
PURPOSE: To determine the effects of each variation in terms of distance, accuracy, etc.

• EXERCISE: Instead of using your putter, kneel at various points approximately ten (10) feet away from the cup on an undulated (uneven) green and roll the ball with your hand into the cup; then accomplish the same thing with your putter.
PURPOSE: Gaining a different feel of the path of the ball to increase your ability to read putts together with their speed and accuracy with your putter.

• EXERCISE: When hitting at the range, continue to relax your grip on the club and consciously swing slowly and easily.
PURPOSE: Obtaining a feel for how relaxing your body enables a greater degree of distance and accuracy as well as allowing the club to do the work by hitting from the sweet spot.

• EXERCISE: Use different grips, stances and distances from the ball with various clubs to deter-

116

mine its effect on striking the ball.

PURPOSE: Using what you learn in situations encountered on the course to improve your game and develop a wide variety of shots to achieve your goal.

• EXERCISE: Place an imaginary club in your hands and practice the smooth, easy, rhythmic movement of hitting a golf ball while focusing on the movement of your shoulders, hips, arms, etc.

PURPOSE: Developing a feel for your proper swing.

• EXERCISE: Always take at least one (or more) long, deep breaths before striking the ball and concentrate on slowing down.

PURPOSE: Learning how to release tension on a regular and consistent basis.

• EXERCISE: Practice swinging any club with your purpose and focus being on maintaining body balance before, during and after the swing is completed.

PURPOSE: Developing a sense of balance to improve accuracy and distance.

• EXERCISE: Freeze your left wrist while putting by holding the club with your left hand and gripping that wrist with your right hand to immobilize it.

PURPOSE: Improving the accuracy of putting by locking in the direction of your control arm to the cup.

• EXERCISE: Instead of spreading your legs while swinging a club, try keeping your feet together while you strike the ball.

PURPOSE: This exercise will force you to dramatically move your hips in unison with your swing to reinforce the importance of a smooth movement that produces a good shot.

• EXERCISE: Invent new games to play while practicing.

PURPOSE: Improving your game relies as much on your imagination as it does on your physical abilities.

• EXERCISE: Use a marker to divide scorecard into six three hole segments.

PURPOSE: Makes round more manageable and gets you mind off of the final result helping you to focus on the task at hand.

• EXERCISE; Hit ten balls with each wedge and write down average full swing carry distances; move ball position forward or back to determine higher or lower than normal shots.

PURPOSE: Gain confidence in any situation involving hazards like wind, water, hidden flags, etc.

• EXERCISE; Addressing an imaginary ball, take your swing but pay attention to whether the full backswing/follow-through allows your body to end up in a balanced position.

PURPOSE: Balance is essential in order to hit

your target.

• EXERCISE; In practice sessions concentrate on the speed of your swing as it affects the length of your swing.
PURPOSE: Your finish should be determined by the rate of acceleration; i.e. the faster your swing, the longer your finish.

• EXERCISE; Make up your own exercises to correct problems.

Relaxation, Visualization and Imagery Training

Can you be psyched & relaxed at the same time?

So, what is the secret to The Mental Side of Golf? There isn't any secret per se but there are elements that are important and necessary to achieve the positive mental attitude that will produce the kind of play that you wish and are capable of performing. This raises a very important question for many of you. You may feel that it is necessary to be psyched up while you are playing a round to perform at your best. Contrary to what you might believe, being psyched up and using relaxation techniques to produce an image of yourself in your mind and seeing yourself performing a shot are possible to coexist.

The use of relaxation, imagery and visualization all need to occur during those times in your play when concentration, focus and staying in your zone are most important. You can use these tools before taking a shot, after you take a shot to examine what went right or wrong, or deal with a problem such as a poor shot, negative thoughts or interfering feelings, These are all examples of when these tools become vital to the golfer. Apart from that, all of the celebrating and psyching that you want can be yours to experience and enjoy. I cannot understand how staying psyched up during difficult shots will make it happen. I disagree with those who believe it will. It seems to me that remaining positive and relaxed is a more important feeling.

**And now, let me introduce you to our training
section. Here you will learn about the positive
function and power that your mind is capable of
and how it can contribute to your excellence of
play.**

Once, when Tiger Woods was struggling with his grip,
he asked his father for some help. His father made some
suggestions, which he tried. When his father asked how
those changes felt, Tiger replied that they felt good. His
father then told him to go out and trust it. Trusting what
feels right is as important a part of any golfer's bag of
tricks as anything else.

Tiger indicated in an interview that he loves working
on his game and forms the attitude that he can be better
tomorrow than I am today. He doesn't have any regrets
for an unsatisfactory performance. He considers the game
of golf a sport and not just an activity. He is both a determined and self-disciplined person.

When asked about how his father's illness affected his
game he said "If you tee it up, you tee it up and give it
everything you have got. That's how I was taught to play
the game and that is how I play the game." He also considers golf very forgiving in that the next day starts a new
game all over again. Basically, his mental attitude is positive and helps him maintain focus and stay in his zone.
The look in his eyes suggests that he is focusing on every
shot before he takes it. And if his visualization and image
of taking the shot is not to his satisfaction, he will back
away from addressing the ball until he is satisfied.

Stephen Ames who hails from Trinidad won the 2006

Players Championship at the Sawgrass TPC course by a six shot margin. He indicated that he had his psychologist with him working on aspects of communication with his caddie, who happened to be his brother. When asked about a particular shot, he replied that "the shot went just as I had pictured it would." He spoke with confidence that what he saw in his mind would indeed be accomplished. In turn, he struck the ball with the same confidence that he experienced when he pictured the shot. In effect, Ames used a technique called imagery and visualization.

This is an extremely valuable tool to help us play the game of golf. I consider imagery and visualization to be one of the most trustworthy tools in your bag.

One of the methods that I was taught to increase my putting accuracy follows. Just after you read the green and address the ball with your putter and as you glance toward the cup, start from the middle of your putter's sweet spot and draw a line with your eyes from that point to the center of the cup in your mind. Do this several times until you have a confident sense or feel for that putting line. This will be the line that will determine distance and direction as well as the degree of impact for you to sink the putt.

This method has really helped me and perhaps it will do the same thing for you. In effect, it is a technique that tends to stimulate your mind to strike the ball with a degree of accuracy, which is then transferred to actually performing the put. The real advantage to this method, which can be used with any golf shot, is that you are able to depend on it consistently.

Granted, the outcome may not be what you would like it to be 100% of the time, but your chances of a positive outcome will be increased dramatically. Again, remember that your mind and body are always connected and sending messages back and forth to benefit you. If those messages aren't benefiting you, you can turn that around to a positive outcome. And remember, it is not circumstance or luck that determines the outcome. It is how clearly you are able to use both sides of your mind to achieve it. It is your mind, learn to use it to your advantage and trust it implicitly.

Sometimes, you may find that you will dream a solution to a problem.

Dreaming dreams allows us to change our reality.

22 Training Exercises

Now I am going to teach you how to experience a state of relaxation. The basis for this exercise can be found in the more complete version entitled *"THE FOCAL STARE METHOD"* in my *"WIN-WINSECRETS"* collection which you can find that on my website.

I have found this technique to be the most intensive and effective one. However, there are several other relaxation techniques that you can try and practice to determine which one works best for you. The more alternatives to relax you can learn the more choices you can make when you want to relax.

Although it is important for you to learn this relaxation method, I am going to place more emphasis on the visualization and imagery training that results from the effects of this exercise. I recommend that you first practice this method while in the privacy of your home or office. This is an exercise just for your mind. After you have mastered the method, I will ask you to use it while practicing on the range. Practice all of your shots on the range before you play a round of golf. Once you've mastered it, the exercise should only take a few seconds for you to perform.

Pick a quiet place in your home or office, sit down and do the following. Sit up straight and make sure that your back and neck are comfortably supported. Hold that position and stare straight ahead at any fixed point in the center of your vision. Focus intently on that point and try not to move your body.

As you continue to stare, you are clearing your body of any tension feelings and your mind of any thoughts that might interfere with relaxing. This will all occur automatically.

Your focus should be on relaxing your mind and nothing else that might be going on in your life. I tell people to let go to help them do this step. Just let go and relax your body and mind. You will be able to feel the difference as you continue performing the exercise.

Now, I want you to slow your breathing down so that it is very comfortable but slower than it is now. If you begin to have difficulty breathing, speed it up a bit. Continue to keep your head and body as still as possible. Take your time. Now quickly check of your body. You don't have to move anything.

Just let your mind start by focusing on your toes and move all the way up to your head to determine whether there is any tension in any of your body parts. If so, let go of it and replace it with the good, soothing feeling of relaxation. That feeling might feel like heaviness or a tingling sensation. I want you to experience as deep a feeling of relaxation as possible. I also want you to experience feeling positive and confident with a clear mind that is open to doing the right thing.

Make sure that you maintain your breathing at a slow, comfortable pace that has a smooth rhythm to it. I want you to feel a sense of balance between breathing, your body and your mind. Just keep staring and all of that will happen automatically. Continue to hold that position for a few minutes to really get a feel for it before you move ahead with the rest of this exercise.

Now as you continue to stare, you will probably find yourself relaxing more and more. Your eyes may become heavy and want to close. That's OK. You can go ahead and close them now. As you find yourself relaxing more and more, go through another body check to determine whether there are any parts that are experiencing feelings of tension. Start with your toes and work up to your scalp making sure that each part is relaxed and tension-free.

Just remain in that state for a few moments more and experience that great feeling. Now, I want you to commit this feeling to your memory so that you can recall it whenever you wish. Remember when I helped you realize that the important part of playing golf is the feeling you have with various shots and with the effective use of all your clubs? Well, relaxation is also a feeling.

As you continue to relax, just as with swinging a club, you will be able to memorize and commit that feeling to your memory. This is very important because I am going to ask you to practice and then later, recall and re-experience that relaxed feeling within a few seconds while you are practicing at the range or on the golf course playing an actual round

What you are doing now is training your mind so that you can become more accustomed to playing your game with a feel for swinging your clubs without having to think about the technical parts of your swing. I don't want you to have to think about how to make a shot. I want you to learn to execute that shot from the feel of having done so successfully in the past.

While you are still in a relaxed state you can experience some imagery techniques. Continue to keep your eyes closed. Imagine that you see yourself taking a 5 iron out of your bag. I am sure that you can remember an instance when you used this club to hit a shot with a near perfect trajectory that landed on the green and backed up to within 10 feet of the cup. Your 5 iron is probably one of your favorite clubs. Imagine that you are back on your course and are about to experience that wonderful shot again. Stand behind your ball and imagine the flight path to the green. Move to the side of the ball. Take two partial practice swings concentrating on hitting down on and through the imaginary ball with the sweet spot of your 5 iron. Now step up to the ball and place the face of your 5 iron behind your ball in a position that is perpendicular to your intended flight line.

Grip your club as you have learned to do during all of your practice sessions. Take your stance and in slow motion execute your golf swing using all of the swing fundamentals that you have engrained in your brain. Pay attention to every aspect of how your swing feels through your complete follow through and as you watch your ball fly to and land 10 feet past the pin and then roll back to stop 8 feet below the pin leaving you an 8 foot slightly uphill putt.

Now I want you to reflect on the mental vision that you caused yourself to experience. Did you actually feel your swing again? Did you enjoy this experience? Now take the time to write down everything that you experienced. Describe your swing mechanics and fundamentals as well as your feelings. Do this stepwise frame by frame and document every detail. By doing this you will not only learn what you have stored in the left side of your brain but you will also begin developing the right side of your brain.

From this point forward pay attention to every detail of your swing fundamentals (left brain activity) and your vision of yourself and your feelings (right brain activity) as you practice each shot. I suggest that your write everything down during or after each session but if you choose not to do this make sure that you have at least catalogued your total experience in the proper location of your brain. It will help you to think about where you are storing your experience as you are storing it.

Now I will give you some homework that will pay great dividends. Think about the best round of golf that you have ever played. If you don't have a scorecard for the course you played, obtain one if you can. The scorecard will help trigger your memory about your most positive golfing experience.

Then I want you to mentally replay your best round of golf using the same procedure that you just experienced with your mental 5 iron shot. Mentally complete one shot at a time for as long as it takes you to document and mentally store everything that you experienced during your best round of golf.

Next I want you to edit your document and make all necessary corrections. You will probably want to check your swing fundamentals references. You may also want to talk with your golf instructor about questions that come to mind as you complete this exercise.

When you have completely documented your best round of golf (It may take you several months to complete this task.) I want you to review your entire round of golf and choose 10 shots that you really want to replay. Then I want you to think about a time when you played similar shots to your satisfaction. Mentally replay the 10 shots that you have chosen and edit your document accordingly.

For the next ten weeks I want you to read and edit your document at least once a week. Make all changes that you believe are required to fully describe all of your left brain and right brain activities.

From this point forward I suggest that you edit your best round of golf document every time you learn something new about swing fundamentals and/or experience a new feeling on a golf course. Continue to do this until you reach the point of diminishing returns.

When you have reached the point of diminishing returns, decide whether it would be valuable to you to do the entire exercise again for a different round of golf. If your answer is yes, do it. If your answer is no, don't do it. In either case you are ready to work on the strategic aspects of your golf game.

Strategic is an adjective that means *"of great importance."* In the game of golf, strategic is best used to modify your plan for conquering a specific course. Strategy is a noun that refers to *"tactical action steps"* that must be completed to achieve a strategic objective. In the game of golf, strategy is best used to modify the mechanical and mental activities that you must complete for each shot.

If you have never played in a golf tournament I suggest that you decide to play in a local golf tournament about two months from now or whenever it is most convenient for you. If you regularly play in golf tournaments, pick the golf tournament that is most important to you.

Obtain a scorecard and yardage book for the course at which your tournament will be played. Go to the course and walk (or ride) the entire course to gain a perspective of what you will experience during the tournament. Take your time and pay attention to every detail of every hole. Stand on every tee. Walk along each fairway. Determine the consistency of the sand that is in greenside bunkers. Look at water and other hazards. Judge the slope and speed of each green. Take copious notes as you walk the course.

After you walk the course, edit your notes while referring to the scorecard and yardage book. Next I suggest that you do some research concerning the history of the course and the course architect.

Now I want you to mentally play the entire course using the following guidelines:

1. Only hit shots that you are fully confident that you can hit well 75% of the time.
2. Only hit shots that you have catalogued in both sides of your brain. This will ensure that you not only understand the proper swing fundamentals for each shot but you are also able to envision each shot.
3. Only hit shots after you have gone through your entire practice regimen.
4. Pay attention to the rules of golf and golf etiquette.

Mentally play the course using the same procedure that you used to document your best round of golf with one major exception. This time I want you to document your most probable shots instead of your best shots. For example, if you usually hit your driver 200 yards and your best drive was about 275 yards, plan on hitting 200 yard drives or less.

Document your entire round of mental golf. Then summarize your plan for each hole in a pocketsize notepad that you will refer to during the tournament. I am sure that you have observed professional golfers refer to their personal notes during a tournament. Your personal notes should also include key points that you learned when you walked the course. Your notepad is your strategic plan for the tournament.

After you have played the tournament, you should take the time to edit your strategic plan for the course to ensure that it is up to date for the next time you play that course.

The mental side of golf requires a lot of challenging and enjoyable work. If it seems difficult to you, you are right. The mental side of golf is difficult but not more difficult than the mechanical side of the game of golf.

If you don't want to make the effort and believe that you can enjoy your golf game by playing the game as best as you can once a month or week, go ahead and do it. That's OK as well.

If the effort that I have described seems interesting to you and you want to begin, then begin as soon as possible. Remember that the left and right sides of the brain are best developed at the same time. Don't forget to clear the left side of your brain with one of your favorite relaxation techniques whenever you begin something new. Also, don't forget to create a vision in the right side of your brain every time you have experienced something that you think is important to retain. Documenting your visions is a challenging task that can be done in seconds but can't easily be accomplished until you train yourself to do it.

Golf's Life Lessons for Children and Adults

I want to say something about the game of golf and the lessons it teaches both children and adults. In the Preface of this presentation, I alluded to my children being quite young when they started playing the game at the ages of eleven and nine. Now they have introduced their children (my grandchildren) to the game of golf at the age of 4 or 5.

Of all of the sports to which parents might expose their children, I have reached the conclusion that the earlier they can be exposed to the game of golf, the better it will be for them. My reasoning is not only so that they will be able to become more proficient at playing the game because of the natural tendencies they possess but also because of the very valuable lessons that the game of golf teaches children. Remember to choose a golf instructor that is capable of teaching good swing fundamentals as well as the mental side of the game. It might be necessary to get a referral to a separate coach, such as myself, who is a specialist in helping with the mental side of the game. These very same lessons can be learned by adults who may have taken the game up much later in life.

Obviously, if you have read or listened to this book, you have noted that I have made constant references to the relationship between the game of golf and life's challenges. As a sport and as a game, your management of golf can help you manage life's experiences. The lessons that are learned in both areas go back and forth affecting each area in a positive manner.

Children and adults learn best when they don't know that they are learning and when they are having fun.

Golf provides this learning and so I devote the next paragraphs to the lessons that can be learned while playing this wonderful and challenging game. All of these lessons have to do with the mental side of the game and are extremely important ones for everyone to learn and retain. Some of these lessons that can be learned while playing the game of golf follow:

Developing a "sense of self": Essentially golf is an individual sport that helps us to learn more about ourselves as we continue to play the game. That learning should be focused on how we *think, feel and act.* The more we can learn about ourselves, the more capable we will become in managing our lives as well as our game.

Learning the value of following the rules: Rules are an essential part of any civilized society and children learning and following them while playing the game of golf will have a direct carryover into other elements of their lives including the development of moral character, which is sorely lacking in our society.

Honesty: Keeping a correct score requires honesty and a solid sense of right and wrong which has an obvious relationship to living life in a forthright manner. The saying goes *"If you cheat at golf, you're only cheating yourself."* Remember that your score is simply an indication of your progress and not a reflection of you as a person. Everyone progresses at a different rate and everyone experiences setbacks no matter how proficient they might become at playing the game.

Integrity: Having integrity in life constitutes having a positive and functional value system as well as the development of qualities that separate those who try to sneak by in dealing with the game of golf or life from those who are not afraid of standing up and being counted. The latter is usually a sign of potential leadership, ultimately resulting in others admiring them and following their example.

Patience: A more mature and healthy method of dealing with life is to postpone instant gratification instead of experiencing instant gratification. Since patience is an essential part of playing the game of golf, the effect of that training on your personal life will become evident and useful over time.

Perseverance: Being able to stay with learning a skill instead of demanding that it be accomplished immediately helps you place trust in the process of learning and the knowledge that results. This requires a sense of developing reasonable expectations of yourself, your ability and your progress in playing the game. In a word, it requires maturity.

Learning how to make effective choices: From club selection to ultimately striking the ball, choices constantly need to be made affecting the outcome and, with more experience, those choices can become more effective, trustworthy and workable. It is said that the most important element in dealing with life has to do with the choices we make on a daily basis. That same sense of effectiveness will be experienced in our personal lives as well.

Goal setting: Learning how to set goals in life is essential in order to grow and progress as well as to experience a sense of satisfaction in having been able to achieve them. Setting goals helps you develop a sense of focus as well as providing the essential elements of staying in your zone.

Learning how to develop strategies: As you learn how to develop strategies in playing golf, doing so for life's challenges will be more common. You can then depend on using that method of strategy development to face and deal with the problems that tend to continuously arise in the management of your life.

Learning how to change strategies in order to adapt to unforeseen situations and circumstances: Despite your game plan, both golf and life require changes to deal with unforeseen circumstances effectively. The winds of change are constantly blowing so that you need to learn to loosen up in order to be able to make changes whenever they are needed. A rigid approach either to the game of golf or to life in general usually leaves us feeling brittle and at the mercy of our insistence that life go our way. Life has its own natural process and although you may believe that you are good at controlling the outcome, you are really not.

Learn about overcoming obstacles: Obstacles constantly present themselves when you play golf. The more prepared you can be to deal with those obstacles, the more effectively you will be able to play the game. The easy way out limits the building of character in life, which is sorely lacking. Golf certainly requires a sense of character on the part of those who play the game and want to progress.

Remaining focused on a task: Learning how to attain and maintain focus in dealing with the various tasks of life helps children who, when they come into adulthood, will be able to deal with boring and mundane elements of life as well as life's challenges. For many adults, that lesson may not have been learned but it is never too late to reinforce that ability. It will pay off whether on the practice range or in the process of playing a round.

Use of gross and fine motor skills: For both children and adults there is a need to use gross and fine motor skills. Because of children's flexibility and greater ease in learning, it is easier for them to adapt to the technical training necessary to play the game of golf. For adults, the learning is a bit more complicated, because they must un-learn some of their gross and fine motor skills to replace them with the skills required to play golf well. It takes a bit of time and effort but the progress made is well worth it.

Positive attitude: To play golf in an effective and enjoyable manner, you must develop and maintain a positive attitude. Otherwise, there will be very little enjoyment or satisfaction be gained. Developing a positive attitude for the game of golf will prove to be very useful in dealing with your life as well. There is a direct relationship between a positive attitude and your ability to perform.

Dealing with stress and frustration: For those who want to play the game of golf well, the need to develop methods of dealing with the stress and frustration that the game brings is essential. Learning stress management techniques in your personal life can help with this process. Becoming angry or discouraged will only bring more problems and interfere with your mental ability to deal with all aspects of the game.

Learning about taking reasonable risks: Taking risks is an essential part of playing golf as much as it is essential in dealing with managing your life. Taking reasonable risks is a necessary element in order to grow and progress in playing the game as well as in dealing with your life. If the fear of taking risks becomes too great, you will end up feeling stuck and frustrated. Since golf is a game that demands taking some risks continuously, learning how to accomplish this process will enhance your personal satisfaction and fun in playing the game.

Confronting fears: Apart from the fear of making mistakes, golf provides ample opportunities to challenge other fears which are the healthiest way of dealing both with the game as well as with life. This is where the saying *Press On!* might have some significant meaning in your life.

Learning about progressing over time: Instead of the instant gratification that many people seek in life, the game of golf demands that you accept that your progress in playing the game will take time, patience and effort to attain a feel for playing the game and enjoying the many benefits that come from doing so.

Developing reasonable expectations for oneself: Instead of searching for perfection, the game of golf teaches you that you shouldn't demand more of yourself than your abilities and progress might allow. It is not making mistakes that become the problem but rather your inability to rebound from them that is the problem.

Developing different perspectives: Playing the game of golf requires a need to view yourself, the course and the game in many different ways. The more alternatives you can develop the more choices you will have, which open up the possibility of becoming more proficient over time. There is always at least one more way to deal with a particular problem.

Recognizing assets and liabilities: Knowing what you are capable of doing or not doing at any point in your progress is very important to advance in the game of golf and life in general. Accepting your humanity helps you to forgive yourself when you make mistakes and will allow you to find ways to rebound from your mistakes.

Learning self-discipline: Self-discipline that is learned while playing golf will give you a sense of structure and help you to develop character and confidence in your life as well. It is a natural way of helping you overcome adversity that is found on the golf course as well as life's challenges.

Dealing with mind sets and slumps: It is not unusual for golfers to experience mind sets or slumps that prevent them from achieving their expectations. These are mental and not physical setbacks that require certain techniques to work through them. Dealing with these issues is very important in the game of golf as well as life in general.

Learning how to focus and stay in your zone: Although it is difficult to focus and stay in your zone, both of these are especially important to the game of golf. Maintaining focus is helped by relaxation.

Learning the difference between thinking and doing: Becoming too heady and preoccupied with the mechanical aspects of the game prevents a sense of fluidity and progress in the game. Golfers who intend to become proficient at the game must also learn to trust their past experiences.

Forming good golfing habits: An understanding of the fundamentals, rules of etiquette and mechanical aspects of the game are essential to play golf and obtain the fullest benefits. Developing a solid practice regimen and learning how to develop the right side of your brain is very important as well.

Developing self-confidence: Developing self-confidence comes from continued practice and the development of a body of knowledge that you can recall to perform well. Understanding that confidence is believing in yourself while believing that what you believe is true helps build self-confidence.

Mind and body control: When you realize that your mind and body are in continuous communication, this will help you develop the controls you need to play and enjoy the game of golf. Without that realization, playing golf becomes a constant struggle to attain what can otherwise be a natural process.

Dealing with winning and losing: In tournaments, winning or losing can be defined by as little as one stroke. Realizing that golf is a game of precision and that a slight error or good shot can make that difference is a sign that a good golfer has learned to accept the ups and downs of the game.

Learning how to test limits: Taking risks and testing limits is an essential part of life as well as the game of golf. Doing so enables growth. In the game of golf there is a never-ending potential for testing to take place. The more fun you can have without taking yourself so seriously, the more growth and knowledge you will be able to achieve.

Learning how to rebound from making mistakes: Making mistakes is an ever-constant part of golf and life but instead of making you angry or discouraged, learning how to rebound and '*PRESS ON!*' will give you a positive outlook, which will help you to build confidence and personal satisfaction.

Dispelling negative thinking in favor of doing something positive: There is no question that negative thinking tends to interfere with performing well. For those of you who are accustomed to this manner of thinking, a refreshing outcome can be experienced if you practice some of the methods outlined in this book. Positive thinking results in positive outcomes.

Learning how to minimize interfering thoughts and feelings: Many people are not aware of the interference that certain thoughts and feelings have in the game of golf and in dealing with life's challenges. Although they may not be able to be totally eliminated, if minimized, the effect will be a worthwhile. The more minimal they become, the greater the chance that you can replace them with thoughts and feelings that will help you.

Trusting ourselves and our judgment: There may be a tendency for you to trust the judgment of others rather than your own. In the game of golf, your judgment is required. Playing golf serves as a training ground for learning how to develop effective judgment that can be trusted. Learning how to do this carries over to handling life's challenges as well.

Developing our own thinking patterns: It is said that when two people think alike, there is not too much thinking going on. Since people generally think differently, rational thought and our ability to envision things must be developed to play the game of golf well and manage our lives effectively. An example of this is the many edits of this book by others helped me create this final edition.

Learning problem-solving techniques: Golf is a sport and game that gives you many challenges or puzzles to solve. Your good judgment is essential to deal with problems and decisions that can't be postponed. The game of golf trains you to develop problem-solving techniques that you can carryover into your personal life.

Developing a feel for our performance: Although the mechanical aspects of the game of golf are essential to play the game with confidence and satisfaction, the mechanical aspects require a great deal of thought and effort. However, with the experience of a solid, repetitious practice regimen, that effort can be simplified by a feel for the game that is similar to learning how to ride a bike. All of this takes time, patience, practice and experience.

Learning about healthy competition: Healthy competition means being able to compete without losing focus on your own game. Focusing on the competition tends to distract you from performing to the fullest extent of their capabilities. Maintaining a sense of staying in your own zone will prove to be very helpful.

Developing an effective practice regimen: Just hitting balls at the practice range will usually not ensure good play on the golf course. A regular and effective practice regimen should always have a plan that deals with both the mechanical and mental aspects of the game of golf.

I am sure that the above list could easily include many other lessons that golfers might add from their own experience. One of the real advantages of the game of golf is that golf is its own teacher. There are many lessons that can be learned from a single practice session and/or one round of golf.

It is important to realize that there is also a mental side to the game of golf. The mechanical aspects of the game of golf are mostly unique to that game. However, the mental side of the game of golf is probably the best method of developing the right side of your brain.

The entire educational system stresses left brain activities to the exclusion of right brain activities. Both left and right brain activities require use for people to achieve their potential. Stephen Covey states in his book "The Seven Habits Of Highly Effective People" that

"All things are created twice. There is a mental or first creation and a physical or second creation. Most business failures begin in the first creation."

Visualization is misunderstood. It is not a spontaneous occurrence that is limited to geniuses, but is instead a normal human function, which uses the right side of the brain to envision a complete picture or vision. The game of golf can teach everyone how to develop the right side of their brain and cycle back and forth between both sides of their brain to achieve their full potential and enjoyment.

And So...
In Closing

And so there you have it. To play the game of golf well you first need to:

1) Gain a basic understanding of the fundamentals of the game of golf,
2) Learn to use both your mind and body to execute various shots,
3) Develop and maintain a solid practice regimen,
4) Develop a feel for your performance while playing.

This involves physical as well as mental activities. Much has been written about the physical side of golf and about swing fundamentals. However, very little has been written about the mental side of golf.

The mental side of golf requires people to develop both the left and right sides of their brain. Since many people have cluttered up the left side of their brain storage with unsorted facts and distractions, I have taught you how to clear the left side of your brain to help you properly sort and catalogue the physical aspects of the game.

More importantly I have introduced you to what you can do to develop the right side of your brain. The game of golf can also help you with all of life's challenges but only if you put the effort into the game.

Enjoy the game of golf. Enjoy yourself and the positive

feelings, confidence and achievement that you are certain to experience. Enjoy your life. **PRESS ON!**

Be aware of the carryover effect from your golf game to other areas of your life. Your ability to focus and stay in your zone will help you minimize the effects of problems that weigh heavily on you.

Don't be afraid of making mistakes or challenging your fears. Instead, focus on how well you can rebound from your mistakes and experience the confidence you will gain from doing so. You can call upon the knowledge that you have gained whenever you take the time to remember how much you have already accomplished and learned in your life. Correcting mistakes if you can and getting on with your life or your golf game is more important than regretting or obsessing about them. Apart from sharpening your mind, the game of golf is to be fully enjoyed.

I would be happy to talk with you personally if it would be helpful. I'm also available for speaking engagements and workshops. In my workshops, you can actually experience many of the techniques that I have introduced in this book. In order to arrange dates for speaking engagements or workshops, you can contact me by e-mail at **charles@charlesmbonasera.com** and I will be happy to get in touch with you.

I also invite you to go to my web site **http://www. charlesmbonasera.com** where you will find several other programs and materials that can help you manage your life in a positive manner, while benefiting your golf game as well.

Other Programs and Books

25

I have scripted and produced 18 CD's dealing with many different stress management issues under the title of **"Win-Win Secrets."**

I also have written a self-help stress management book with 3 CD's entitled **"Guide To A Life Management Process."** It contains my own working model of how to identify and deal with stress patterns effectively.

I have written the book **"How to Stay Well and Live Life to the Fullest,"** which is a compilation of many sayings and mini-stories accumulated over the years of my practicing psychotherapy that provide an incentive for changing negative patterns in our lives...

Presently, I am working on writing the book **"How in the Hell Did This Happen to Me?"** that will deal with patterns, which we have brought from our childhood into our adult lives that do not work as well as they once did. It will identify many of those patterns by offering case studies as well as methods of changing them.

As a result of potential emotional damage to children in competitive sports, I am also planning to produce a CD and book combination guiding parents into the world of their children's participation in organized, competitive sports in a healthy manner.

I will be having a chatroom and blog dealing with the mental side of golf and other sports as well as with life management issues. These are free services on my website and I welcome your participation. Further information and the dates when these new materials will be available appear there as well.

I trust you have enjoyed this book and will be aware of and practice the suggestions I have offered in order to deal with the mental side of golf as well as your life. I am sure that practicing them will enhance both your golf game and your life.

Enjoy Your Game. Have Fun. Enjoy Your Life, Stay Well and PRESS ON!

Developing a Sense of Humor

I believe that one of the main ingredients that will both save us from bad shots and games as well as preserve our sanity in dealing with the game of golf is to develop and maintain a sense of humor. Over the years, I have collected a few jokes and stories that have helped me accomplish those ends and so I am passing some of them to you. Most of these were obtained from friends in the form of e-mails. I cannot remember who all of them were but whoever they are, they deserve a round of applause.

A Clubhouse Story

Several men are in the locker room of a private golf club. A cell phone on a bench rings and a man engages the hands free speaker-function and begins to talk. Everyone else in the room stops to listen.
MAN: "Hello"
WOMAN: "Honey, it's me. Are you at the club?"
MAN: "Yes"
WOMAN: "I am at the mall now and found this beautiful leather coat. It's only $1,000. Is it OK if I buy it?"
MAN: "Sure, .go ahead if you like it that much."
WOMAN: "I also stopped by the Mercedes dealership and saw the new 2006models. I saw one I really

liked"
MAN: "How much?"
WOMAN: "$90,000"
MAN: "OK, but for that price I want it with all the options."
WOMAN: "Great! Oh, and one more thing ... The house I wanted last year is back on the market. They're asking $950,000"
MAN: "Well, then go ahead and give them an offer of $900,000. They will probably take it. If not, we can go the extra 50 thousand if it's really a pretty good price."
WOMAN: "OK. I'll see you later! I love you so much!!"
MAN: "Bye! I love you, too."
The man hangs up. The other men in the locker room are staring at him in astonishment, mouths agape.....
He smiles and asks: "Anyone know who this phone belongs to?

Investment Mergers

Here are some solid investment tips that every-one should heed in order to "make a killing" in the market. Although most of them have not taken place yet, keep your eyes open so that you can get in on the ground floor when they do.
1.) Hale Business Systems, Mary Kay Cosmetics, Fuller Brush, and W.R. Grace Co. will merge and become:
Hale, Mary, Fuller, Grace.

2.) Polygram Records, Warner Bros., and Zesta Crackers join forces and become:
Poly, Warner Cracker.
3.) 3M will merge with Goodyear and become:
MMM MMM Good.
4.) Zippo Manufacturing, Audi Motors, Dofasco, and Dakota Mining will merge and become:
ZipAudiDoDa.
5.) FedEx is expected to join its major competitor, UPS, and become:
FedUP.
6.) Fairchild Electronics and Honeywell Computers will become:
Fairwell Honeychild.
7.) Grey Poupon and Docker Pants are expected to become:
Poupon Pants.
8.) Knotts Berry Farm and the National Organization of Women will become:
Knott NOW!
9.) Victoria's Secret and Smith & Wesson will merge under the new name:
Titty Titty Bang Bang

And finally, here are some

GOLFISMS

• Don't buy a putter until you have had a chance to throw it.
• Never try to keep more than 300 separate thoughts in your mind during you swing.

- When your shot has to carry over a water hazard, you can either hit one more club or two more balls.
- If you are afraid a full shot might reach the green while the foursome ahead of you is still putting out, you have two options: you can immediately shank a lay-up or you can wait until the green is clear and top a ball halfway there.
- No matter how bad you are playing, it is always possible to play worse.
- The inevitable result of any golf lesson is the instant elimination of the one critical unconscious motion that allowed you to compensate for all of your many other errors.
- If it ain't broke, try changing your grip.
- Everyone replaces his divot after a perfect approach shot.
- A golf match is a test of your skill against your opponents luck.
- It is surprisingly easy to hole a fifty foot putt for a 10.
- Counting on your opponent to inform you when he breaks a rule is like expecting him to make fun of his own haircut.
- Nonchalant putts count the same as chalant putts.
- It is not a gimme if you're still away.
- The shortest distance between any two points on a golf course is a straight line that passes directly through the center of a very large tree.
- There are two kinds of bounces; unfair bounces and bounces that go just the way you meant to play it.
- You can hit a two acre fairway 10% of the time

and a two inch branch 90% of the time.

• If you really want to get better at golf, go back and take it up at a much earlier age.

• Since bad shots come in groups of three, a fourth bad shot is actually the beginning of the next group of three.

• When you look up, causing an awful shot, you will always look down again at exactly the moment when you ought to start watching the ball if you ever want to see it again.

• Every time a golfer makes a birdie, he must subsequently make two triple bogeys to restore the fundamental equilibrium of the universe.

• If you want to hit a 7 iron as far as Tiger Woods does, simply try to lay up just short of a water hazard.

• To calculate the speed of a player's downswing, multiply the speed of his back-swing by his handicap; e.g., back-swing 20 mph, handicap 15, down swing = 300 mph.

• There are two things you can learn by stopping your back-swing at the top and checking the position of your hands: how many hands you have, and which one is wearing the glove.

• Hazards attract, fairways repel.

• You can put a draw on the ball, you can put a fade on the ball, but no golfer can put a straight on the ball.

• A ball you can see in the rough from 50 yards away is not yours.

• If there is a ball on the fringe and a ball in the bunker, your ball is in the bunker. If both balls are in the bunker, yours is in the footprint.

- It's easier to get up at 6:00 AM to play golf than at 10:00 AM to mow the yard.
- Sometimes it seems as though your cup moveth over.
- A good drive on the 18th hole has stopped many a golfer from giving up the game.
- Golf is the perfect thing to do on Sunday because you always end up having to pray a lot.
- A good golf partner is one who's always slightly worse than you are. That's why I get so many calls to play with friends.
- That rake by the sand trap is there for golfers who feel guilty about skipping out on lawn work.
- If there is a storm rolling in, you will be having the game of your life.
- Golf balls are like eggs. They are white. They are sold by the dozen and you need to buy fresh ones each week.
- A pro-shop gets its name from the fact that you have to have the income of a professional golfer to buy anything in there.
- It's amazing how a golfer, who never helps out around the house, will replace his divots, repair his ball marks, and rake his sand traps.
- If your opponent has trouble remembering whether he shot a six or a seven, he probably shot an eight (or worse).
- It takes longer to learn to be a good golfer than it does to become a brain surgeon. On the other hand, you don't get to ride around on a cart, drink beer, eat hot dogs and fart if you are performing brain surgery.
- Years ago, when it became necessary to change

from bifocals to trifocals, I was concerned about my game. Upon asking a friend what he thought would happen to my play with the new lenses, he replied "It will probably be the same as before you made the change." I'm still not sure whether that was a compliment.

Testimonials

From a Practicing Attorney and Coach:

I have known Charlie Bonasera for over twenty years. Over that time I have had the pleasure of seeing and experiencing his system of inducing better play and greater enjoyment from sport.

As a coach of three U.S. National and thirteen New York State championship hockey teams I am well aware of the importance of the mental side of sport. It could easily be argued that once certain fundamental skills are achieved, most games are played from the neck up. Most would agree that golf is a sport that a good mental attitude is crucial to success but I believe that the performance of virtually any athlete in any sport can be maximized with a better mental approach to the game and to the inevitable stress moments the sport produces.

It is in teaching others how to mentally focus and to produce results in tight situations that Charlie Bonasera has become adept. I watched his work in the Buffalo New York area and had the fortunate circumstance to work with him in my own golf endeavors. I was very pleased with the results obtained personally and know of many others who felt they had greatly improved as well.

We all want to improve but most of us have neither the athletic ability nor the time to devote to our avocations to achieve the results we believe we are truly capable of.

Learning how to maximize the mental aspects of what we do, however, is both attainable and realistic for even the weekend warrior and will produce better game results and a feeling of satisfaction.

I would strongly endorse the "Bonasera method" and know that those who take to heart the contents of his book will find their own sport a more fulfilling and rewarding experience.

Pat Rimar, Practicing Attorney and Coach

From a Former Competitive Skater:

I thought about writing this testimonial long and hard before being able to sit down and actually write it. There is one thing that keeps coming to mind of my work with Mr. B during my skating career. He became an asset to my skating as well as my life as I now know it. During many competitions, somehow I never skated as well as I could. He taught me various relaxation and imagery techniques but the one that always stays with me is actually very simple, namely visualize what you do best and then do it!

Lake Placid was a very special place for me for it was there that the Olympic spirit came through whether you were there for the 1980 Olympic Hockey team's victory over the Russians or after that emotional time. When you walked into that arena you could feel the magical aura. A few years after those Olympics I was competing in a regional figure skating competition. I knew what I needed to do, but was fearful that it would not turn out as I wanted. Mr. B realized my preoccupation and helped me to overcome it.

About an hour before taking the ice, he took me to a

dressing room and walked me through a visualization of skating a flawless program. When I closed my eyes I was in the arena all alone on the ice. When I stepped onto the ice and looked around there were no judges, coaches or spectators so there was no one to please but myself.

I visualized myself on that ice skating the perfect program and after I finished I bowed to the empty seats, turned towards the entrance and standing there was the one person that I knew would not judge me whether I skated well or "wiped the ice". That person was there holding a single long red rose. As I skated closer the image became clearer. That person was my dad.

What Mr. B was showing me was that the perfect program was really about pleasing myself because the image of my dad there holding that rose demonstrated that no matter what I accomplished I needed to do my best and make myself proud instead of being concerned about others. There is no such accomplishment as a perfect program. However, those who loved me would be there for support no matter what the outcome. An hour later I went out and skated one of the best programs of my life. When I finished, I looked up in the stands and there, standing all alone at the very top was my dad with thumbs up because he knew that I could do it.

That moment will always live in my heart. And now after several years and events in my life like getting through a test in school or giving birth to my two beautiful children, when I question if I can do it I still visualize that skating program with my dad standing at the end of the ice with a single long stem rose. Then I just do it.

Christina Togni, Businesswoman and
Former Competitive Figure Skater

From the Skating Pro Who Got Me Started:

As a skating director and teaching professional, I have been actively involved in skating for approximately 50 years. During that time I have been instrumental in introducing many additions to the sport. One of them was the importance of sports psychology. Teaching ice skating consists of two parts: the technical aspect and the human aspect.

As my students graduated to top competition, I realize there was a need, not only to train the body but the thought process as well.

It was because of this that I contacted Mr. Bonasera and interested him in working with my competitive students. Athletes who work on the mental aspects of their performance start a very important process. They begin to realize how powerful the mind is. If the mind and body are trained simultaneously and are in sync with each other, then the mind frees the body to do what it needs to do.

I have trained two national champions. The success with my students was greatly enhanced with my work with Mr. Bonasera. His work became a very important part of their training.

Frances Duroure, Specialist in Coaching and
Administration of Figure Skating Programs
Amherst N.Y., St. Petersburg, Florida
Madeira Beach, FL

From a Former Golfing Client:

I wanted to tell you how pleased I was with the progress of my golf game since I worked with you. Although it's been several years since we consulted, I'm still practicing

159

their game.

One of the first things about golf that my fraternity brother told me is - keep an accurate score. If you got a seven that is what you record - I will not think highly of you if you tell me you got a five when I know you got seven – please be honest.

Dan Regelski, MBA
Regional Small Business Development
Center Director,
Florida Gulf Coast University, Fort Myers, FL

From A Professional Athlete:

Charlie asked me to read his book, The Mental Side of Golf, to get a reaction from a former professional athlete. I'm not a big book reader but I did crack it open on my recent vacation cruise. I played baseball for a living and was fortunate to be able to compete at a professional level. I started my career in the Minors with the Buffalo Bisons, Charlie's home town team. I ended my professional career playing third base for the Toronto Blue Jays.

Now, I'm not an experienced golfer but I play in a number of charity tournaments. The points that The Mental Side of Golf makes about the importance of the mind impressed me the most. It doesn't make any difference what sport is being played. In my case it was baseball but basketball, hockey, and certainly golf requires the effective use the mind in order to play a sport consistently well.

If an athlete is fortunate enough to have natural ability that would certainly provide an opportunity for him or her to enter into a professional level. However, ability alone will not sustain an athlete's career over a span of time. A few of my coaches in the big leagues often make sure that we, as a team, knew that physical ability gets you there but it's what's between your ears that keeps you there. That advice helped my game go from being a good baseball player to being named a two time All Star. How athletes in whatever sport use their minds to their advantage in playing their game is very important. Professional athletes don't only have to be consistently good at their sport and play hard, they are in need of a good game plan and also have to play smart. They also need to have a feel for the sport they play.

This point has to do with how effectively athletes use their minds and Charlie emphasizes this throughout his book. He likens the most effective use of a person's mind to the mind of a child who believes that can do anything and whose persistence is usually met with success. I know that I can attribute my success as a pro ballplayer to the principles that Charlie points out in his book and I would heartily endorse those principles for everyone who plays sports.

I also enjoyed the frequent comparisons that he made between the training and importance of self-discipline necessary both to play golf and in dealing with life management. I agree that how an athlete lives his or her personal life reflects on how well that athlete will perform in their sport.

Kelly Gruber, Former Third Baseman for the Toronto Bluejays, Two Time All Star, Sarasota, FL

From An Entrepreneur And Successful Bussinessman:

Although I'm not a golfer...I play squash...I decided to read Charles' book THE MENTAL SIDE OF GOLF" anyway.

I have been playing against an opponent for some while whom I could not beat on the court. After reading about half of the book, I was able to beat him by one point. The next week, I read the second half of the book and I won once again. I'm convinced that the focus of the book on the effective use of the mind was instrumental in my improvement in play. I would highly recommend that everyone read the book to learn more about the principles and training techniques that Charles offers to improve the use of the mind in whatever endeavor in which they might engage.

John Greer, President of
US Credit Liquidators,
Facilitator,
Young Entrepreneurs of Sarasota, FL

From A Retired Policewoman:

I have just finished reading **"The Mental Side of Golf"** by Charles M. Bonasera. This is a book I will re-read many, many times because although an avid golfer, I am not a particularly good golfer.

The book will not teach you how to play the game but will help you achieve the highest level of skill, enjoyment and competition. The book reinforces what I already know but seldom take the time to recap before playing. Just reading the book brings back memories of all my practice sessions, lessons and wonderful shot experiences. It made me take a forward look at myself by visualizing making that excellent shot the last time I played a particular hole.

The book points up the fact that mentally, the more aware I can become of aspects of my life, think about the situation at hand and then move ahead, the result will be more fulfilling and satisfying.

Why is it that I might usually top the ball off the first tee sending it only 100 yards to the left? It's my "mental side" which the book points up so well. When I perform the exercise described in the book to visualize my next shot, the problem is most often corrected so as not to repeat the problem once again.

Everyone can "stay in the zone" and that is why I loved this book and I know that any golfer, young or old, can enjoy reading and learning how to challenge and improve the "mental side" of their game. This is a Win-Win book to read time and again. It is a great gift to enjoy as I did.

Paula Shingfield, Retired Police Officer, LAPD,
North Port, FL

From A Retired Businessman

I enjoyed your book. You did a great job getting the golfer to focus on the mental side of the game. Reviewing past shots and using your relaxation techniques before taking shots was excellent. I was able to visualize my problems and using the suggestions presented in the book. The instructional part was very helpful!

Al Cloutier, Retired Business Executive

From A Cosmetologist:

Congratulations on your publication!! I want to order the book with the CD's and would like to know if I could order directly from you and receive an autographed copy?

I also have someone in mind that it would be the perfect gift. I don't golf with him so I won't have to worry about him beating me at my own game!

Joette Ianonne, Cosmetologist, Amherst, NY

From A Former Caddy:

As a boy, I caddied at a private club for a group playing for money, were up tight and not having any fun.. The psychology of the game becomes more difficult when expectations fall short. Golfers may see their game as a personal reflection of themselves when beaten. The approach some take can be self-defeating. Your book clearly addresses and helps golfers realize how their expectations can become a "make or break" aspect of their game and their lives.

Dan Rapp, Retired Business Executive

Printed in the United Kingdom
by Lightning Source UK Ltd.
129614UK00002B/76/A

9 780980 137378